# Christian INITIATION
## A JUNIOR HIGH CATECHESIS

By

James Bitney

GENERAL EDITOR
Rev. Gerard P. Weber, S.T.L.

CONSULTING EDITOR
Irene Murphy

BENZIGER PUBLISHING COMPANY
Mission Hills, California

**Student Illustrations: Page 7** Floriene Tracy Lagunero, 17 years; **Page 17** Marisha Scott, 15 years; **Page 27** Margaret Galileo, 16 years; **Page 35** Phung Huynh, 17 years; **Page 37** Jenna Miyahara, 17 years; **Page 38** June Tanasuwankasem, 14 years; **Page 40** Phung Huynh, 17 years; **Page 45** Roxanne Sterling, 17 years; **Page 47** Linda Joo, 17 years; **Page 48** Gina Galileo, 14 years; **Page 57** Janine Harispe, 16 years; **Page 67** Nadine Romero, 17 years; **Page 92** Lisa Mori, 17 years. These illustrations were created in 1995 by students from Immaculate Heart High School, Los Angeles, California.

**Illustrations: Page 8** John Burns; **Page 9, 10, 16** Mark H. Adams; **Page 18** GTS Graphics, Inc.; **Page 19, 26** Mark H. Adams; **Page 28** John Burns; **Page 29** Mark H. Adams; **Page 30** John Burns; **Page 36, 39, 46, 49, 56** Mark H. Adams; **Page 58** Ann Clark; **Page 59** Father Solanus Guild; **Page 61** GTS Graphics, Inc.; **Page 66** Mark H. Adams; **Page 68** Ann Clark; **Page 76** Mark H. Adams; **Page 77** John Burns; **Page 85** Mark H. Adams; **Page 86** GTS Graphics, Inc.; **Page 90** Ann Clark

**Photography: Page 4** Tony Freeman/PhotoEdit; **Page 4** James L. Shaffer; **Page 5** Alan Oddie/PhotoEdit; **Page 6** Mary Kate Denny/PhotoEdit; **Page 13** Myrleen Ferguson Cate/PhotoEdit; **Page 14** James L. Shaffer; **Page 15** FourByFive; **Page 20** Robert Brenner/PhotoEdit; **Page 22** David Young-Wolff/PhotoEdit; **Page 23** Myrleen Ferguson Cate/PhotoEdit; **Page 24** Jeff Greenberg/PhotoEdit; **Page 25** David Young-Wolff/ PhotoEdit; **Page 30** Superstock (Four By Five); **Page 31** Tony Freeman/PhotoEdit; **Page 32** James L. Shaffer; **Page 33** James L. Shaffer; **Page 35** Myrleen Ferguson Cate/PhotoEdit; **Page 40** Alan Oddie/PhotoEdit; **Page 42** Myrleen Ferguson Cate/ PhotoEdit; **Page 43** Myrleen Ferguson Cate/PhotoEdit; **Page 45** Michael Newman/ PhotoEdit; **Page 50** Tony Freeman/PhotoEdit; **Page 51** Ann Clark; **Page 51** James L. Shaffer; **Page 52** Tony Freeman/ PhotoEdit; **Page 53** Herbert Lanks/Superstock; **Page 54** James L. Shaffer; **Page 55** Alan Oddie/ PhotoEdit; **Page 60** Father Solanus Guild; **Page 62** Tony Freeman/PhotoEdit; **Page 62** Stephen McBrady/PhotoEdit; **Page 63** Tony Freeman/PhotoEdit; **Page 63** Tony Freeman/PhotoEdit; **Page 64** Tony Freeman/PhotoEdit; **Page 65** Myrleen Ferguson Cate/PhotoEdit; **Page 69** Rembrandt van Rijn, *Return of the Prodigal Son,* St. Petersburg, Hermitage, Courtesy of Scala/Art Resource, NY; **Page 70** Myrleen Ferguson Cate/PhotoEdit; **Page 71** Myrleen Ferguson Cate/PhotoEdit; **Page 72** FourByFive; **Page 74** Alan Oddie/PhotoEdit; **Page 75** FourByFive; **Page 78** FourByFive; **Page 82** James L. Shaffer

**Cover Photograph:** Mazer Corporation

**Nihil Obstat:** Rev. Frederick F. Campbell

**Imprimatur:** †John R. Roach
        Archbishop of Saint Paul and Minneapolis
        March 17, 1995

The *nihil obstat* and *imprimatur* are official declarations that a book or pamphlet is free of doctrinal or moral error. No implication is contained therein that those who have granted the nihil obstat and imprimatur agree with the contents, opinions, or statements expressed.

Scripture passages are taken from the *New American Bible with Revised New Testament.* Revised New Testament of the New American Bible, copyright © 1986 by the Confraternity of Christian Doctrine. All rights reserved. Old Testament of the New American Bible, copyright © 1970 by the Confraternity of Christian Doctrine, Washington, D.C. All rights reserved.

Send all inquiries to:
**BENZIGER PUBLISHING COMPANY**
15319 Chatsworth Street
Mission Hills, California 91345

Printed in the United States of America.

ISBN 0-02-655944-7 (Student Edition)
ISBN 0-02-655945-5 (Catechist Edition)

1 2 3 4 5 6 7 8 9   WEB   99 98 97 96 95

# Contents

# ANSWER THE CALL

"Hey, you! Yes, you. Come here. I have something I want to **talk** to you about—right now!"

If the speaker of those words were your principal, the call might have you shaking in your shoes. You might be wondering if you had done something wrong. (And if you *had* done something wrong, you might be wondering if you are about to get caught.)

"Hey, you! Yes, you. Come here. I have something I want you to **do**!"

If your mother or father said those words to you, you might be thinking about a long Saturday morning of sweeping, vacuuming, mowing, or raking. Or worse! You might be thinking about having to take care of your younger sister or going over to old Aunt Florence's house or heading to the supermarket with a long list in your hand.

"Hey, you! Yes, you. Come here. There is something I want you to **be**!"

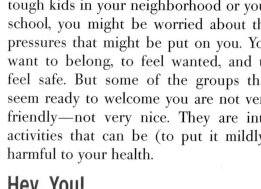

If those words came from one of the tough kids in your neighborhood or your school, you might be worried about the pressures that might be put on you. You want to belong, to feel wanted, and to feel safe. But some of the groups that seem ready to welcome you are not very friendly—not very nice. They are into activities that can be (to put it mildly) harmful to your health.

## Hey, You!

Believe it or not, somebody is calling you. That somebody is asking you to **listen** to a very important message—a message that

will make a difference in your life forever. If you listen, understand, and believe the message, you will change.

That same somebody is asking you to **do** something—something challenging and real. You are being invited to live with courage and with character. You are being asked to choose the right way over the wrong way.

And that same somebody is asking you to **be** somebody. If you answer the call, you will belong to a group that can change the world. You are asked to be part of a group that is stronger than any gang, more powerful than any team. Yet, that group can be warm, welcoming, and supportive to you your whole life long.

This is a religion class, right? So, by now you know that the one who is calling you is Jesus! For two thousand years, Jesus has been calling young people just like you to belong to the Family of Faith. All you have to do is answer the call.

## Different Journeys

Everyone's faith journey is a little different. Some people were baptized as babies. After that, they may have not had the chance to be a part of the Family of Faith. Now, for one reason or another they are on the way back.

Some young people are thinking of becoming members of the Catholic Church for the first time. That's great! They will have lots of questions. They might be a little scared of what will happen.

Some young people have missed receiving First Communion or Confirmation. Now seems like a good time to get back on board. Parents or friends or classmates might have invited these young people to catch up.

Some young people have been members all along, but the early teen years seem like a good time to get a handle on what Catholics believe, celebrate, live, and pray.

No matter which of these journeys you are on, the next few weeks are going to be exciting and important ones for you.

# Christian Initiation

This book is a chance for you to answer the call of Jesus. The title of the book means that nobody becomes a Christian all at once. You are initiated into membership. This initiation has three basic steps:

> Baptism
> Confirmation
> Eucharist, or Communion.

You are going to be learning or reviewing these steps in the weeks to come. Maybe, at the end of that time, you will be taking one or all three of these steps. You will also be learning about the importance forgiveness plays in the Family of Faith. Finally, you will be given a clear and simple overview of how Catholic Christians follow Jesus. If you let it, that little overview will be part of you for the rest of your life.

You are not going through this experience alone. Not at all! You are being supported and helped by your teachers or youth ministers. You are even going to be helped by your peers. Your peers are very important when it comes to answering the call of Jesus.

Here are a few hints that will help you as you go through this book together:

1. *Listen!* Be open to what you read and hear.
2. *Share!* Be willing to let your teachers and classmates know what you think and what you feel.
3. *Connect!* Try to see how what you are learning connects to your everyday life.
4. *Try!* You will be learning ideas, attitudes, skills, and actions. Don't be afraid to try out what you are learning.
5. *Support!* People who follow Jesus help one another. As you go through this experience of Christian Initiation, be sure to support one another.

If you manage to do those five things as you learn, you will not only enjoy what you are learning, you will also have something to carry with you through the tough days ahead.

And Jesus himself is going to be with you because he is the one who is saying: "Hey, you! Yes you. Come here, I want you to belong to my group! You are always going to be my friend."

So, answer the call!

# TELL YOUR STORY

**God has given you a new birth—a living hope!**
*(Rite of Baptism)*

# WHO ARE YOU, ANYWAY?

Here is a chance for you to identify yourself in just the way you want to be identified. Below is your personal file. Within that file, put as much information as you can cram into the space. (You won't be marked for neatness, so draw, color, or use abbreviations.)

List your name (the way you like it), the music you like, the foods that make you drool, what you hate, your favorite color—just cram your folder full of **you**!

# PERSONAL STORIES

**Be honest!** You have watched those television shows where people tell *everything*, haven't you? Most people love to listen to stories about the troubles and joys other people have. If you have ever kept a diary, spent time journaling, or swapped stories about yourself with your friends, you are one of those who love personal stories.

Everybody has a story to tell. Personal stories show values, hopes, and dreams. Personal stories reveal who people really are. The next story is a bit of fantasy, but it will help you get the idea. (You might also uncover some things about the life of Jesus you will want to ask about later.)

## Whose Story?

Once upon a time (or so a legend has it), the Lord God—Holy and Blest!—wanted to make sure that the story of Jesus got written and got written right. So the Lord God—Powerful and Abiding!—sent an angel to a scribe to guide him through the story.

The angel told the scribe what the Lord God—Wise and Wonderful!—had in mind and asked if he wanted the job. The scribe jumped at it. And why not? After all, it's not every day that you get the Lord God—Marvelous and Fabulous!—as a client.

So the scribe took his pens, his ink pots, and his paper under his arm. The angel took the scribe under its wing. And off they both went to find and follow Jesus, and to record all that He said and did.

## Joy and Favor

The angel whisked the scribe to a stable in Bethlehem, then to a sheep-dotted hillside that lay under an angel-crowded sky. The scribe paid attention, met with great joy, and scribbled down what he met.

In an instant, the angel transported the scribe into the desert, where he witnessed Jesus in a devilish duel. The scribe paid attention, met with great courage, and scribbled down what he met.

## Wisdom and Power

Scarcely before the scribe could work up a thirst, the angel sailed him to the banks of a river. Jesus rose dripping from its waters, glistening like the sun. The scribe paid attention, met with great favor, and scribbled down what he met.

Next, the scribe found himself sitting on the angel's shoulders. All around was a great crowd of people. They were all listening intently as Jesus spoke of new creation, new heavens, new

earth. The scribe paid attention, met with great wisdom, and scribbled down what he met.

Suddenly, the scribe felt seasick. He was astride the angel's back, who was hovering a few feet above a raging sea. A tiny boat bobbed in the waters' cauldron. Jesus stood in the prow. At His word, the sea relaxed, and the waters pulled themselves tight like a bed sheet around the sea's corners. The scribe paid attention, met with great power, and scribbled down what he met.

## Welcome and Forgiveness

Then, the scribe was walking fast to keep up. The angel was behind him, urging him along. Jesus was ahead, inviting everyone to follow. And follow they did: the rich and the poor, the lame and the limber, the young and the old—like guests heading for a banquet. The scribe paid attention, met with great welcome and forgiveness, and scribbled down what he met.

## Generosity and Sacrifice

The shadows lengthened. The oil lamps were dimming. The special meal was all but complete. Then, with a bittersweet smile, Jesus lifted a loaf of the unleavened bread, broke it, gave it to His friends, and said, "My children, this is My body. Eat it, and I am with you."

The scribe watched in awe as Jesus then lifted the wine-filled cup, gave it to His friends and said, "Behold this wine so red and good, it is My blood. Drink it, and I am with you." The scribe paid attention, met with great generosity and sacrifice, and scribbled down what he met.

## Sorrow, Love, and Belonging

Suddenly, the scribe was standing at the foot of a cross, holding his breath. The angel stood by weeping. Jesus hung on the cross and breathed his last. The scribe paid attention, met with great sorrow, and scribbled down what he met.

The scribe's eyes were glowing. The stone rolled away. The angel bowed low. Jesus' tomb was empty. The scribe paid attention, met with great love, and scribbled down what he met.

Candles flickered. Hands were uplifted in prayer. Bread was broken and shared. Wine was poured out and drunk. Jesus was not there, yet He was present. The room was filled with strangers, but no one was an outsider. The scribe paid attention, met with great belonging, and scribbled down what he met.

## What a Life!

Finally, the scribe was finished. He dotted the last *i*, crossed the last *t*, and blotted the ink from his fingers. Gazing over the scribe's shoulder, the angel finished reading the story the scribe had written.

"What a fantastic story!" the angel shouted. And the scribe said, "Indeed."

"What a wonderful life!" the angel cried. And the scribe said, "Absolutely."

"Surely, this is exactly what the Lord God— All-knowing and All-seeing!—had in mind!" the angel declared. And the scribe said, "To be sure."

"Yes, the Lord God—Grand and Glorious!— is going to love it!" the angel cheered. And the scribe said, "Hurrah!"

"What a plot! What a hero! This has got to be the greatest story ever told!" the angel exclaimed. And the scribe said, "Amen."

"From now until forever," the angel said grandly, "any who hear will know that *this* is Jesus' story." But the scribe said, "No way."

The angel looked shocked.

"What are you talking about?" the angel demanded. "Of course it's Jesus' story."

The scribe looked like a new person.

Gazing calmly into the angel's fiery eyes, he said, "This isn't Jesus' story. It's mine. I wrote it!"

For a moment, all was silent. Then there was heard the voice of the Lord God—Awesome and Majestic! "At last," the voice thundered, "you—*both of you*—got it right."

## Questions

◆ Why did the angel insist the story was Jesus'?
◆ Why did the scribe insist that the story was his own?
◆ Why did God agree with both of them?

## Read and React

Read the two paragraphs below. After each paragraph, in your own words, respond to what you have read.

Christians have a deep-seated and constant hunger to be part of the story of Jesus, to find their place in it. The tale of the angel and the scribe reveals that the story of Jesus really is your story. It becomes yours whenever you join to share stories about who you are with others who have encountered the story of Jesus and are striving to live it out in their own lives.

If you think your story has little to do with the story of Jesus, remember this: Jesus' story does not become your story by some kind of magic. It happens by *conversion* (a big word for personal change.) Meeting the story of Jesus dares you to decide, to profess your faith that you are not all there is, that you are a part of—not apart from—other persons and things. It challenges you: "Will you respond in love to Jesus who is love, or not?" If you say yes and give in to the power of love, that's conversion. Then, Jesus' story becomes your story. And your story becomes a love story, too.

# THE LOVE STORY BEGINS

**Y**our personal story begins the day you left your mother's body and wriggled your toes in the wonderful light of day. Your faith story begins with a kind of birth, too. Jesus told his first followers to "make disciples of all the nations. Baptize them in the name of the Father, and of the Son, and of the Holy Spirit" (MATTHEW 28:18–20).

Your part in Jesus' love story begins at the baptismal font, where you celebrate your conversion—your giving in to the power of God's love in the **Sacrament of Baptism.** What makes you so special to be called to the baptismal font? *Nothing!* Baptism is not about being special, it is about being **welcomed.**

## Welcome

At the celebration of Baptism, the priest or deacon welcomes you by marking you with the sign of the cross, calling your name, and saying:

> The Christian community welcomes you with great joy. In its name I claim you for Christ our Savior by the sign of His cross. I now trace the cross on your forehead, and invite your parents and godparents to do the same.          (*Rite of Baptism,* 79)

When you answer the call to follow Jesus, the cross becomes a birthmark for you. It reminds you of the way Jesus identified Himself with you through His death on the cross of Calvary. The cross reminds you that Jesus won the fight over sin and death, and the sign of the cross is your share in that victory. The cross welcomes you and identifies you as one of Christ's own. That is why the cross is one of the most treasured symbols Christians have.

## The Story of Jesus

Okay, you have been welcomed and marked with the cross. Now what happens? You turn your attention to the story of Jesus who died on the cross. You listen to a reading of God's Word from the Bible. The message is just for you, so pay special attention.

Any of the Scripture passages listed below may be read at the celebration of Baptism. Use your Bible to look up two of the passages. Listen as the two readings are shared. In the box, draw a personal symbol of what you hear:

ROMANS 6:3–5          MARK 1:9–13
GALATIANS 3:26–28     JOHN 7:37–39

CHRISTIAN INITIATION

## Faith Shared

Baptism is not a solo flight. You are called to belong to a whole community of people. This circle of believers who have joined their stories to the story of Jesus prays for you and wants to share your story.

Inspired by Jesus who overcame death on the cross, and supported by the community of believers, you are asked to make a three-fold rejection of sin and anything else that may keep you from overcoming death with Jesus and the community of saints:

1. "Do you reject sin so as to live in the freedom of God's children?"
   **"You bet I do!"**
2. "Do you reject the glamour of evil and refuse to be mastered by sin?"
   **"You bet I do!"**
3. "Do you reject Satan, the father of sin and prince of darkness?"
   **"You bet I do!"**

Are you beginning to see what your Baptism story is all about? Being a follower of Jesus is definitely serious business. It is real life, and you won't find it on a game cartridge or on your television screen!

## I Believe

Finally, you are asked to profess your faith—your belief in God. The words you use to tell the world about your belief are hundreds of years old. You see, the profession of faith is not just something personal. It is a short story of trust that is shared by all who are part of the family of faith.

1. "Do you believe in God, the Father almighty, creator of heaven and earth?"
   **"You bet I do!"**
2. "Do you believe in Jesus Christ, his only Son, our Lord, who was born of the Virgin Mary, was crucified, died, and was buried, rose from the dead, and is now seated at the right hand of the Father?"
   **"You bet I do!"**
3. "Do you believe in the Holy Spirit, the holy catholic Church, the communion of saints,

the forgiveness of sins, the resurrection of the body, and life everlasting?"
**"You bet I do!"**

4. "This is our faith. This is the faith of the Church. We are proud to profess it, in Christ Jesus our Lord."
   **"Amen!"**

## Death and Re-birth

When you approach the font of Baptism, the waters recall all your washings, growth, deaths, and comings to life.

You are covered with waters. In that plunge, something drowns and dies—selfishness. You just can't put yourself in the number one spot again—not without remembering you are supposed to be different. The priest or deacon calls your name and says: "I baptize you in the name of the Father, and of the Son, and of the Holy Spirit."

That did it! You are changed. Maybe you don't feel anything, but you are now filled with God's own energy. That energy has a name—the Holy Spirit—the power of God present in all the people who are Church. You came out of the water with a guarantee that you are not alone in life, that you do not have to count only on yourself to live out the faith you have professed. You

# THE LOVE STORY BEGINS

have new life and the Holy Spirit and a caring community to help you live that life.

## Oiled and Wrapped and Full of Light

To finish off the celebration, you get a spot of blessed oil rubbed on your forehead. The oil, called *Chrism,* reminds you that you belong to Jesus Christ.

Inside and outside you are a new creation. So, you receive a white garment as a sign of that newness. The white garment says that you are honored members of the Church. It reminds you that we are "clothed in Christ" from head to foot.

Christians are not simply light-carriers like people who might carry a flashlight into a darkened cave. Christians, as Jesus Himself reminds us, are light itself: "You are the *light* of the world" (MATTHEW 6:14).

So, you receive a lighted candle. With your parents and godparents—indeed, with all the Family of Faith—to support you, you can let your light shine, and "walk always as a child of the light." (*Rite of Baptism,* 110)

## Questions

◆ What is one way you have been blessed?
◆ Who has helped support your faith? Who has gotten you this far?
◆ How can you use your faith to be a light for others?
◆ How can you support the faith of others?

## Read and React

Read the two paragraphs below. After each paragraph, in your own words, respond to what you have read.

Baptism celebrates your becoming a new creation, a person reborn into a new relationship. In Baptism, God's own Spirit fills you with new life, makes you a "Spirited" person for others, and sets you on the way of Christ. Baptism welcomes you as a blest member of God's holy people, the Church, where you can continue to shine and make your story part of Jesus' story of loving service—the greatest story ever told.

_____

_____

The profession of faith called a *creed* sums up the story of God's great adventure on earth. Like a love story, it details God's passion for people. In your profession of faith, meet God head on and give yourself to the God who cares, the God who is your loving parent, your redeeming Lord, and your life-sustaining energy. You declare that your faith is a faith shared with others, a faith in which you can grow and be supported by the faith and concern of others.

_____

_____

CHRISTIAN INITIATION

# BAPTISM:
## *Believe and Celebrate*

These two pages are a chance for you to pull a few things together, telling your story and the story of Jesus together.

## SHARE

Choose one or more of the share activities below. Remember, each of these activities is for sharing with others.

1. *Write Your Story:* Begin by thinking of a title that describes a personal talent, trait, or interest. For example, if you value animals and like to take care of them, your title might be: *The Cat's Meow*.

   Next, create a subtitle. Think of the qualities that you admire in yourself: what you stand for, your strengths, for example; a sense of humor, compassion, strong-mindedness, athletic ability, etc. Use these qualities in your subtitle.

   Finally, write your story. Start with just a paragraph or two. Write anything you want. It's your story. If you need some ideas to get started, try writing about:

   ◆ the family you come from
   ◆ who your parents are
   ◆ something you did that made you feel proud
   ◆ the first place you remember living in
   ◆ how an important time, event, or person has affected you

2. *Make a Life Map:* On a sheet of newsprint, draw a map of your life, from your birth to the present. To make the map:

   ◆ draw a time line
   ◆ put events in chronological order
   ◆ include simple illustrations
   ◆ insert captions

   Include anything on the map that you feel is significant for telling the story that is you, for example: your first day of school, a move your family made, or a death in the family.

3. *Jesus' Story:* With the help of one of the real scribes of Jesus' life (Matthew, Mark, or Luke) put together a short story of the life of Jesus and then describe your own belief in Jesus. Use some of the same techniques you might have used to describe your own life.

# ACTIVITIES

Pick one or more of the following actions to help bring your story and the story of Jesus together.

1. Read a chapter of one of the Gospels every day for a week. Take notes on what you read.
2. Search for an illustration of Jesus that really appeals to you. This can be a realistic picture or a symbol (such as the cross). Display this picture in your bedroom.
3. Talk to one friend about your Christian Initiation journey. Talk to a friend who is *not* in this class with you.
4. Visit a church. Don't do anything special there. Just open your heart to the story of Jesus.
5. Write the following words on a slip of paper or a card: "Jesus, your life story is my life story." Put the paper where you are sure to find it someday this week.

## Pray

The prayer below is the Apostles' Creed. It is a very ancient summary of what the followers of Jesus believe. Pray the creed together. Try to say this creed every day for a week. Try, too, to really *mean* what you are saying.

### The Apostles' Creed

I believe in God, the Father almighty, creator of heaven and earth.

I believe in Jesus Christ, His only Son, Our Lord.
He was conceived by the power of the Holy Spirit and born of the Virgin Mary.

He suffered under Pontius Pilate, was crucified, died, and was buried.

He descended to the dead.

On the third day He rose again.

He ascended into heaven, and is seated at the right hand of the Father.

He will come again to judge the living and the dead.

I believe in the Holy Spirit, the holy catholic Church, the communion of saints, the forgiveness of sins, the resurrection of the body, and life everlasting. *Amen!*

CHAPTER  **2**

# SHOW THE WAY

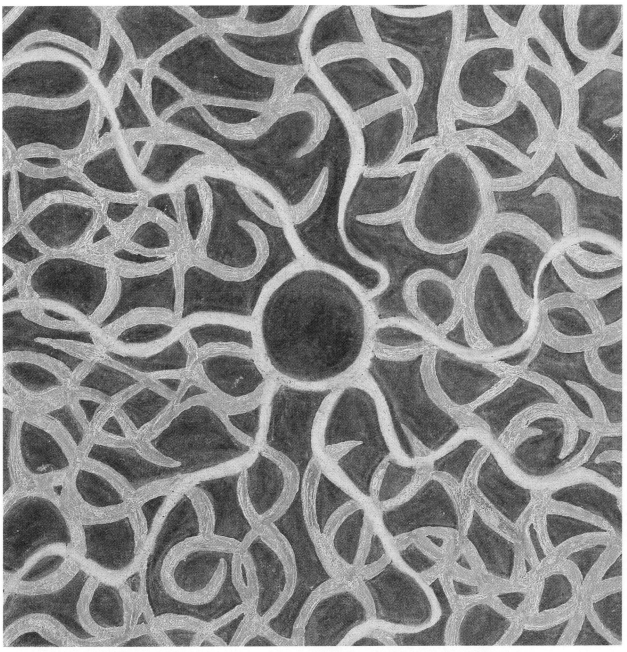

**Bring them into your holy, catholic, and apostolic Church.**
(*Rite of Christian Initiation*)

# WHAT WILL YOU BECOME ?

Jesus told His followers to teach people "to carry out everything I have commanded you. And know that I am with you always, until the end of the world" (MATTHEW 28:20).

It is pretty hard to think about the end of the world, but you can dream about the future—your future. On the star chart below, write at least five things you would like to do or become in your future. Then write at least five things that you would like people to see in you in the future.

# *Live* CARING SERVICE

**B**eing baptized "in the name of the Father, and of the Son, and of the Holy Spirit" means entering into the grand and glorious relationship that is God. Baptism assures you that God knows how much you want to belong, to be welcomed, and to be united with one another. The story of Jesus made this clear.

Jesus spent His life among real people, welcoming them into His family. Jesus welcomed the disappointed to delight, the frail to fitness, the outcast to acceptance, the sinful to salvation, and the excluded to God's embrace. He encouraged everyone to rejoice in the Good News that believing in Him and making His story their own meant a growing relationship and belonging with God:

> Whoever puts faith in Me believes not so much in Me as in the one who sent Me, and whoever looks on Me is seeing the one who sent Me. (JOHN 13:45–46)

Jesus did more than welcome and encourage people to follow Him to a relationship with God. Jesus cleared the way. He blazed a trail and paved it with service and caring. Following Jesus means that you share the story of Jesus by the way you live. The story below shows just what that means.

## The Jacket

The grey-haired man examined his reflection in the clouded mirror. The letter jacket fit him just right, and it was warm. He turned to the right and ran a gnarled hand over the blue

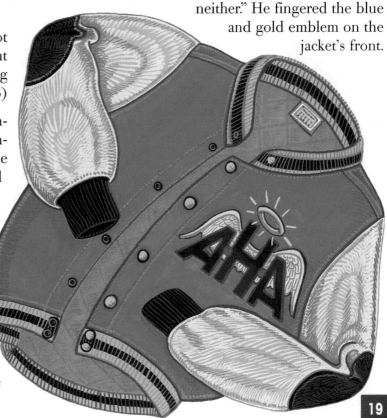

leather sleeve, which was emblazoned with a volleyball insignia.

"Hmmm," the old man murmured, "I played some *football* in my day. I could tell you a story about football, that's for sure."

"Tell it," said Darrah Stevens, the girl who was helping him. "I'd be pleased to hear it."

Given that simple invitation, the old man launched into a tale of his high school days, fifty years ago in North Dakota. He spoke of his play on the varsity team and how he was forced to leave school when World War II began.

"Left high school the summer before my senior year," the old man said wistfully. "Never got to finish." Then, admiring the jacket in the mirror again, he went on, "Never got one of these neither." He fingered the blue and gold emblem on the jacket's front.

"What's this *A.H.A.* stand for?" the old man asked.

The girl smiled and said, "It stands for Academy of the Holy Angels. It's a school near here."

The old man stuffed his hands in the jacket's pockets—deep, and fleece lined. "I don't know," he mused. "What do you think?"

"Hey, it looks great!" Darrah said. "I know you were looking for something else, but it's the only winter jacket we've got left. Besides, you were an athlete. It belongs on you. Take it."

The old man looked at the young woman, smiled, and winked, "I think I'll do just that. Thanks."

"No," said the young woman. "Thank *you*. Come visit us again. You're always welcome."

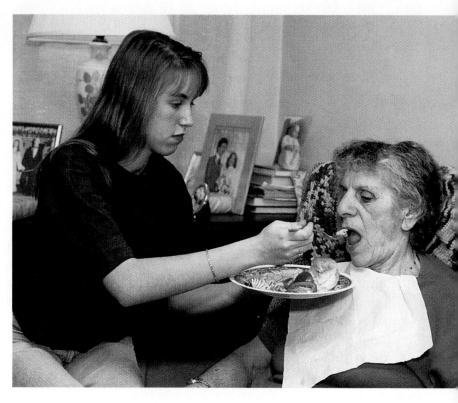

The old man opened the door of the Free Store, squared his drooping shoulders, and trudged out into the cold Minnesota air.

## At Your Service

The Free Store, located in a run-down part of a large midwestern city, is a shop where people who cannot afford to buy what they need can come and get clothes, shoes, dishes, and some small appliances for free. Darrah Stevens, a high school senior, works there two mornings a week as part of her high school's Christian service program called "The Baptismal Lifestyle."

In the beginning, Darrah had offered to volunteer at the Free Store mainly because she figured it would get her out of class. However, after being there for over two months, her reasons for staying had changed.

Darrah expected the Free Store to be like a regular store, but when she got there, she found it a much more depressing place. Many of the customers seemed to feel embarrassed or angry at having to be there. At first Darrah couldn't understand this. Later, she figured that she would probably feel embarrassed or angry, too, if she *had* to shop there.

At first, Darrah put on a cheery kind of false front for the customers at the store. But after a while, she realized that her act was phony, and that it showed. So she decided instead to be herself—a little laid back, but welcoming.

At first, Darrah waited on her Free Store customers without really relating to any of them. She saw them as sort of faceless, all the same. Gradually, however, Darrah began to notice how each person was an individual. She stopped looking through them and started to make connections, even if they were brief ones. She realized that the most important part of her job was simply to make people feel welcome and comfortable.

"I figured it was important to treat others with honor by remembering that each person is

# CARING SERVICE

special," Darrah said. "I figured it was important to make our customers feel welcome, like they belong."

After the old man left, proudly sporting the letter jacket, Darrah attended to three other customers. As the last one left the store, Darrah heard the sound of a car's horn honking. She called out to Sister Jane, the nun who ran the Free Store, "Hey, Sister, I gotta split. My ride back to Holy Angels is here. See you on Friday."

"Darrah, wait!" Sister Jane called as the girl headed for the door. "Where's your letter jacket?"

"Don't worry, Sister," Darrah replied. "It's where it belongs."

## Questions

- How was Darrah living out her Baptism?
- Do you think Darrah's actions lived up to the name of her high school's Christian service program ("The Baptismal Lifestyle")? Why or why not?
- What is one way you can care for and serve others?
- What would you like to add to the story? What would you like your "chapter" in the story to be called?

## Read and React

Read the section below. After you read it, respond by filling out your own "Baptismal Lifestyle Pledge."

As an infant, Darrah Stevens was baptized and welcomed into the community of the Church. Darrah's work at the Free Store is one way she is living out her Baptism by welcoming others, serving others, and engaging them in caring relationships. Your Baptism makes you a welcoming, storytelling, faith-filled, reborn, blest, and Christ-wrapped light for the world. Your caring service can extend to others the welcome and belonging you experience.

Make *your* Baptism more real. You ought to have your own Baptismal Lifestyle Pledge.

### TO LIVE OUT MY BAPTISM, I PLEDGE . . .

To welcome others by _____

To share the story of Jesus by _____

To bless others by _____

To act as a light for others by _____

# PUT HEART AND SOUL INTO IT

## Christians have a splendid story to share,

a story whose "once upon a time" stretches back to the very dawn of creation. Filled with fantastic characters and events, the story's plot winds its way through the lives of a chosen people, comes to a crescendo in the life, death, and resurrection of Jesus, then continues along through the Christian era, gathering as it grows the wisdom, tradition, rituals, and lived experience of the Church. Like all great stories, the story is not finished; it's still being written, still being told. To be complete, it needs *your* story lived out in caring service.

Over the centuries, people have joined in relationship to serve and care as Jesus did. This relationship is called Church—the joyful community that shares God's life with one another and welcomes others into that relationship. Caring service is what baptized people do.

### A Prayerful Promise

Baptism sets you on a course of caring service. That's why your journey just *starts* at the baptismal font. It doesn't end there. Baptism begins the story. It's not the whole story. Baptism is a promise, not fulfillment. Baptism is for growth in belonging, in relationship, in service, and in sharing with others. Jesus gave a special lesson in that service on the evening before He died. His lesson had two parts—serving and praying:

> Jesus picked up a towel, tied it around himself, poured water into a basin, and began to wash the feet of His followers. Afterward, Jesus said, "Do you understand what I just did for you? If I just washed your feet—I who am Teacher and Lord—then you must wash each other's feet. What I just did was to give you an example: as I have done, so you must do."
>
> (JOHN 13:4–6, 12, 14–15)

After the Apostles' feet were cleaned, Jesus lifted His eyes and talked directly to God the Father:

Father, the hour has come. Give glory to your son that your son may glorify you, just as you gave him authority over all people, so that he may give eternal life to all you gave him. Now this is eternal life, that they should know you, the only true God, and the one whom you sent, Jesus Christ.     (JOHN 17:1–3)

By living what you believe and by having a personal relationship with God and Jesus, the only Son, you show other people the story of Jesus alive and well in everyday life. The water poured over your head in the sacrament of Baptism marks you as one of God's own. You are a living page of the Gospel, and you may be the only Gospel some person in your life will ever read.

## Just Do It

The teenager asked the old nun, "How can I learn to pray?"

The nun's response was worthy of a television ad for athletic shoes. "Just do it!" she tossed back with a smile and a twinkle in her eyes.

Praying is really no big deal. You could pray right now if you really wanted. Here is a little plan to help you:

1. *Get quiet.* It is hard to contact God (or for God to contact you) when you are noisy inside.
2. *Read God's Word.* Pick a favorite verse or two and read them slowly and carefully.
3. *Let your heart do the talking.* Try not to ask for favors. Just talk to God from your heart in your own words.
4. *Let your heart do the listening.* God does not have an answering machine, fax, or computer terminal. Answers to your prayers are found in the same place you found the words to use for talking to God.
5. *Change a bit.* The more you talk to God, the more you will change for the better. You will be kinder, more understanding, less selfish.

# PUT **HEART** AND **SOUL** INTO IT

Don't ever be afraid to pray. There are many ways to get in touch with God. Christians pray in groups or all alone. There are formal prayers and simple gasps. There are prayers that happen on sad days and on happy ones. Most of all: **Just do it!** It is part of answering God's call—part of belonging to God's Family. It is part of being the baptized you!

By your Baptism, you are invited to put your heart and soul in to everything you do!

## Questions

◆ Can you name three ways your parish washes feet—that is, serves others? How does this service show the story of Jesus to others?

◆ What are the names of two or three people you know who serve and care for people? What do their actions teach you about your Baptismal Pledge?

◆ In your own words, what is prayer?

◆ What happens to you when you try to pray? (Be honest! Prayer can be tough sometimes.)

## Read and React

Read the two short passages from God's Word. On the lines, write the words that come to your heart when you read God's message.

Through faith you are all children of God in Christ Jesus. For all of you who are baptized into Christ have clothed yourselves with Christ. There is neither Jew nor Greek, there is neither slave nor free person, there is not male and female; for you are all one in Christ Jesus.                          (GALATIANS 3:26–28)

_____

_____

Those who accepted the message were baptized. They devoted themselves to the teaching of the Apostles and to the life of the community, to the breaking of the bread and the prayers. All who believed were together and had all things in common. They ate their meals with joy and sincerity of heart, praising God and enjoying favor with all the people.          (ACTS OF THE APOSTLES 2:41, 42, 44, 46–48)

_____

_____

# BAPTISM:
## *Live and Pray*

R E V I E W

These two pages are a chance for you to go over just how you can live the story of Jesus and how you can answer the baptismal invitation to pray.

## SHARE

Choose one or more of the share activities below. Remember each of these activities is for sharing with others.

1. *Share Some Scripture:* Share at least two of the readings below. They are sometimes suggested as readings for the celebration of Baptism. Talk over what the readings might mean. Don't be afraid to ask for help if you have some trouble understanding what you uncover in the readings. (Remember, you will be learning what it means to follow Jesus throughout your whole life.)

   ◆ ROMANS 6:3–5 (new life in Christ)
   ◆ MARK 1:9–13 (the baptism of Jesus)
   ◆ JOHN 7:37–39 (streams of living water)

2. *Make a Plan:* In groups of two or three, make a plan for living out a Baptismal Pledge by serving others. How would you go about doing this anyway? Talk about how you can make people feel good when you serve them, but how that might also make them feel bad. How do you feel when somebody helps you? Start by listing ways you are already helping others—at home, in school, with your friends, or even at church.

3. *Find a Living Gospel:* Look for people whose actions show their baptismal commitment. They don't have to be big, important people. They could be saints or they could be people who live on your own block. Tell their story, and show how—by looking at the way they live and act—you can discover more about following Jesus Christ.

4. *Share a Prayer:* Either as a class or as a small group, get together and try to pray together. Remember, you learn to pray by praying.

# ACTIVITIES

Pick one or more of the following actions to help you live and pray the story of Jesus.

1. Pore over newspapers and magazines to find some examples of living gospel stories—people who by their actions share the story of Jesus.

2. Listen to some of your favorite music. Between songs, look in your heart to find out if your music helps you get in contact with God or if it gets in the way. Start keeping a Baptismal Pledge "top 40" chart. List those songs that help you serve others or help you pray.

3. Set aside three minutes a day for the next week to let your heart do some talking and some listening. You will be surprised at what you say and what you discover.

4. Some time during the next week, turn off the radio, television, stereo, CD player, or electronic game system and read something from the Gospel of MARK.

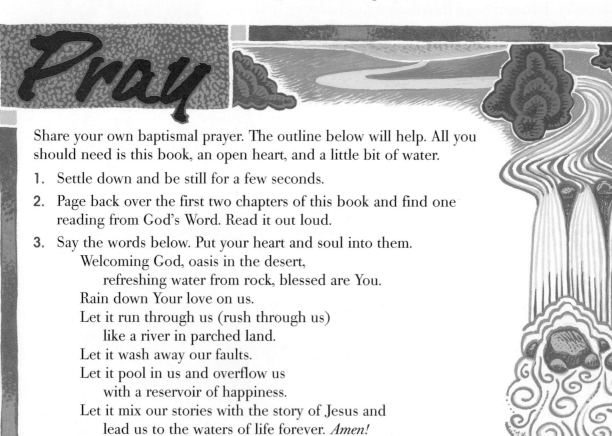

## Pray

Share your own baptismal prayer. The outline below will help. All you should need is this book, an open heart, and a little bit of water.

1. Settle down and be still for a few seconds.

2. Page back over the first two chapters of this book and find one reading from God's Word. Read it out loud.

3. Say the words below. Put your heart and soul into them.
   Welcoming God, oasis in the desert,
       refreshing water from rock, blessed are You.
   Rain down Your love on us.
   Let it run through us (rush through us)
       like a river in parched land.
   Let it wash away our faults.
   Let it pool in us and overflow us
       with a reservoir of happiness.
   Let it mix our stories with the story of Jesus and
       lead us to the waters of life forever. *Amen!*

4. To conclude, use some water on your fingertips, mark yourselves with the sign of the cross, and say:
   In the name of the Father, and of the Son, and of the Holy Spirit, let this water remind us of the welcoming love of God. Let it refresh us and strengthen us to serve and care as Jesus did. *Amen!*

CHRISTIAN INITIATION

CHAPTER **3**

CATCH
THE
SPIRIT

**Now you will receive the power of the Holy Spirit!**
*(Rite of Confirmation)*

# THE THIRD PERSON

Christians sign themselves with a cross and call on the names of Father, Son, and Holy Spirit.

## Who is that Third Person—the Holy Spirit?

Take the Holy Spirit pop quiz below. Then, get ready to learn about the Holy Spirit and the second sacrament of Christian Initiation, Confirmation.

◆ **First,** circle one word in each of the pairs.

I think the Holy Spirit is more like . . .

| | |
|---|---|
| past | present |
| wind | fire |
| open | closed |
| inside | outside |
| old | new |

◆ **Second,** agree or disagree with each of the statements below.

**YES    NO**

☐ ☐ I think faith in the Holy Spirit isn't as necessary as faith in Jesus.

☐ ☐ I think only certain people can experience the Holy Spirit.

☐ ☐ I think that you don't really need the Spirit.

☐ ☐ I think that the Holy Spirit gives different gifts to different people.

☐ ☐ I think the Holy Spirit can give us power.

◆ **Third,** write about one way you think the Holy Spirit might have gotten through to you so far in your life.

_____

_____

_____

CHRISTIAN INITIATION

# COME, HOLY SPIRIT

Have you ever wondered who the Holy Spirit is, anyway? What is the Holy Spirit like? If you have, you're not alone. When asked what the Holy Spirit meant to him, a young person getting ready to celebrate Confirmation wrote the following. Check it out.

## The Rush

My father's 1951 Chevy was sprung like a cheap bunk bed. It swayed and creaked even when standing still. It shook our back teeth when it idled. It thrilled us to the bone when it ran the hilly, three-mile dirt road that led into town.

We called the journey "the roller coaster." Of course, we had never been on a true roller coaster and could make no authentic comparisons, as if that mattered. And we knew that no fancy thing-a-ma-bob on rails could touch the thrill of our "roller coaster."

Up and over, careening and crunching, plunging and climbing the hilly, rough sand road, spitting gravel like a watermelon eater spits seeds, we'd speed our way. I remember the intense thrill in the stomach's pit as the battered car flew down then—quick!—up the hills. I remember the blueberries, growing wild, that lined the rough road. No, that's wrong. I remember the *blur* of blueberries as the skyrocketing car rushed past. I remember the static crackle of the car radio, too stupid to know that no music could compete with the song beating inside us.

But most of all, head stuck out the back door window, mouth open in an almost painful whoop of joy, I remember the roaring rush of wind. It pushed our eyes open wide, as if to say, "Look! Don't blink! You'll miss something wonderful!" It stung our faces and reddened our cheeks with the delight of the day. It surged in our ears, saturating them with sounds as deep as the sea. It transformed our hair into streamers, kite tails, comets. It shocked us and filled us with the fiery oxygen of unfettered joy. It animated us and made us bounce in our seats, jump in our skins.

"More, more, more!" we'd shout. And the wind greedily swallowed and granted our pleas in its exhilarating and spirited rush.

## The Power of the Holy Spirit

Before the first moment, all that might be, could be, should be, was but a thought tucked in the mind of God. Before the first moment, time was not and confusion was. Before the first moment, all was in darkness. Before the first moment, the earth was only a void, covered with waters that swirled and raged.

Then, at the first moment, the Holy Spirit, like a brooding dove, hovered lovingly. The Holy Spirit transformed the darkness into light and life. Like a steadying wind, the Holy Spirit calmed the molten seas. From the first moment, the Holy Spirit never stopped coursing through creation. Throughout history, the Spirit touched the lives and hearts of individuals, filling them with the power of God's love.

# COME, HOLY SPIRIT

Till, at last, that Spirit came upon one who would bring about a whole new creation.

Jesus returned in the power of the Spirit to Galilee. He came to Nazareth, entered the synagogue on the sabbath, and was handed the book of the prophet Isaiah. Jesus read this passage:

I am filled with the power of the Holy Spirit. Yes, God's own Spirit has anointed Me and sent Me to bring glad tidings to the poor, to proclaim liberty to those who are captives, to give sight to the blind, to unshackle the prisoners, and to announce a time of favor and blessing from the Lord.

Then Jesus said, "These words from Scripture are a promise from God. Today, that promise is fulfilled in Me."

(Adapted from LUKE 4:14–21)

From that moment on, through, with, and in Jesus, the Holy Spirit blanketed the land with new life, with a reason for faith, with the promise of freedom, with justice and love, with welcome and forgiveness, and with power. That power became yours on the day of Pentecost.

## Questions

◆ How did the young person in the story of the old Chevy experience the Holy Spirit?

◆ To what did the person compare the Holy Spirit? Do you think that image of the Spirit is a good one?

◆ Can you recall any instances in the Bible that might describe the Spirit in the same way this story did?

◆ What is your image of the Spirit?

## Read and React

Read slowly through the passage below. Then, write a short profession of your own faith in the Holy Spirit.

Suddenly, from up in the sky, there came a noise like a strong, driving wind. Tongues as of fire appeared, which parted and came to rest on each of them. All were filled with the Holy Spirit. They began to make bold proclamations as the Spirit prompted them (ACTS 2:2–4). At Pentecost (fifty days after Jesus' resurrection), the Holy Spirit came to make hearth and home not in an individual, but *in a people,* a community, a Church. From the moment Jesus' first followers received the Spirit, they were empowered to welcome others into the Spirit's embrace. They did this by drawing on Jesus' own actions—baptizing and the laying on of hands (ACTS 8:15–17; 9:17–19).

# Celebrate

# REJOICE IN THE POWER

In the waters of Baptism, by the power of the Holy Spirit, people "die and rise" with Christ—sharing in His death and resurrection. In the laying on of hands (now called Confirmation), people share the power of the experience of Pentecost—enabling them to live, witness to, and share new life with others.

Confirmation is linked to Baptism. Like Baptism, Confirmation is a sacrament for growth, a sacrament that creates the Church and helps it grow—helps *you* grow. Confirmation grafts you to the believing community that first bloomed at Pentecost—to the Church that is for the service of others. Confirmation welcomes you into a community that is Spirit-filled. Confirmation welcomes and commits you personally to a mission of caring service.

## Followers of Jesus Celebrate

The story of Jesus clearly demonstrates that He rarely passed up an opportunity to celebrate with people. (Take a minute to look up the passages listed below. They are very interesting and fun to read.)

- When Jesus invited others to follow, and they left all to do just that, Jesus celebrated (LUKE 5:27–35).
- When Jesus wanted to teach a lesson about hospitality, He regularly couched His message in terms of a feast (LUKE 14:7–24).

- When Jesus spoke of God's welcoming and forgiving love, He spoke of rejoicing shepherds, happy housewives, or feasting fathers (LUKE 15:1–31).
- Likewise, when Jesus was near the end of His ministry, He chose to gather His friends to share a festive meal that we continue to celebrate down to this day (1 CORINTHIANS 1:23ff).

Jesus used celebration—the beautiful language of festival—to express the *meaning* of what he was doing and talking about. In celebration, Jesus expressed and confirmed the existence of the ever-present, but habitually hidden and unspoken, presence of God. But Jesus did even more in His celebration. He not only

expressed God's love, but actually brought it into being. The followers of Jesus all celebrate! Together!

Note the emphasis on *together*. Like all other sacraments, the celebration of Confirmation is a celebration *of a people*. In the celebration, the people called Church, re-discover the heart of what it means to be a community of witnesses filled and empowered by the Holy Spirit. The Holy Spirit comes not only to fill the hearts of those confirmed, but also to enlarge the hearts of all the Church by including new members.

Confirmation celebrates:

♦ being empowered
♦ being gifted
♦ being equipped for witness and service
♦ being part of the whole People of God

## Celebrating Confirmation

Most often, a bishop presides at the celebration of Confirmation. The bishop is the spiritual leader of a section of the Church called a diocese. The bishop's presence and leadership are a reminder that all Christians are connected to the Apostles at Pentecost. After the Apostles received the Holy Spirit, they immediately gave the Spirit to others through the laying on of hands. (*Rite of Confirmation*, 7)

The celebration takes place during the Mass to remind us of three important realities:

1. Baptism and Confirmation lead to Eucharist.
2. Eucharist (First Communion) is part of our welcome and initiation into the Church.

3. The same Holy Spirit who "lifts you up" at Baptism and who empowers you at Confirmation also makes Christ present in the Eucharist, all in order to bring you closer to God. (*Catechism of the Catholic Church*, 737)

Here is how the celebration of Confirmation works:

***God's Spirit-filled Word:*** The celebration begins with the sharing of God's Word. The readings remind all the people that no one can really know the Father or the Son without the Spirit. The Spirit reveals God's Word and gives the power to welcome that Word in faith. It is the Holy Spirit who joins your story to the story of Jesus, as Saint Paul says, "No one can say: 'Jesus is Lord,' except in the Holy Spirit" (1 CORINTHIANS 12:3).

# REJOICE
## IN THE POWER

*Presentation and Instruction:* In response to God's Word, the candidates for Confirmation are presented to the bishop. The bishop then speaks briefly about the great gift of the Holy Spirit. He invites the candidates to commit themselves to the mission and ministry of the Church.

*Renewal of Baptismal Promises:* The bishop invites the candidates, their sponsors, and all present to renew the promises they made at Baptism and to profess their faith—the story of trust that is cherished and shared by all who are Church.

*Laying on of Hands:* The bishop prays that the same Spirit who gave the candidates new life in Baptism will now come to empower them with spiritual gifts. Then the bishop and priests lay hands on the candidates by extending their hands over them. Ever since Pentecost, this powerful gesture has signified the gift of the Holy Spirit. (*Catechism of the Catholic Church,* 1298)

> All-powerful God, Father of our Lord Jesus Christ, by water and the Holy Spirit you freed your sons and daughters from sin and gave them new life.
>
> Send your Holy Spirit upon them to be their helper and guide.
>
> Give them the spirit of wisdom and understanding, the spirit of right judgment and courage, the spirit of knowledge and reverence. Fill them with the spirit of wonder and awe in your presence.
>
> We ask this through Christ our Lord.
>
> (*Rite of Confirmation,* 42)

*The Anointing with Chrism:* The candidates with their sponsors approach the bishop. The sponsor places a hand on the candidate's shoulder in a

gesture of support. The bishop lays his hand on each candidate's head and anoints the forehead with chrism in the sign of the cross. Remember, the cross is our birthmark. This signing recalls the signing we experience in Baptism. The bishop calls the candidate by name and says:

"Be sealed with the Gift of the Holy Spirit."
The newly confirmed person responds:
**"Amen."**

*The Sign of Peace:* Finally, the bishop shares a sign of peace with the newly confirmed. The bishop says:

"Peace be with you."
The newly confirmed person responds:
**"And also with you."**
This recalls the risen Lord's greeting and the outpouring of the Holy Spirit on His followers at the first Easter:

> On the evening of the first day of the week, Jesus' fearful followers had locked the door where they were staying. Suddenly, Jesus came and stood before them.

# REJOICE
## IN THE POWER

*Celebrate*

"Peace be with you," He said. At the sight, the followers rejoiced. Then Jesus said, "As the Father has sent Me, so I now send you." Finally, Jesus breathed on His followers and said, "Receive the Holy Spirit." (From JOHN 21:19–23)

The sign of peace also shows that the newly confirmed are now in union with the bishop and all others in the Church, and are ready to join in communion around the Lord's Table. (*Catechism of the Catholic Church*, 1301)

Like Baptism, Confirmation leans to and yearns for communion (unity). Confirmation isn't for itself. Like Baptism, Confirmation is for Eucharist.

That is the simple and wonderful celebration of the power of the Spirit in life—the sacrament of Confirmation.

## Questions

- How do you share "power" with others? Think for a minute—this is a tough one!
- What kinds of celebrations are most important to you? Talk about them in some detail.
- Why do you think that the laying on of hands is such a powerful and empowering gesture?

## Read and React

Read the two paragraphs below. In your own words, respond to each paragraph on the lines provided. What do these words mean to you *right now*?

Confirmation celebrates your full entry into the Church. It is your public testimony that you accept God and God's community accepts you. Now you have a responsibility to live in such a way as to show what you believe and what you have celebrated.

_____

_____

_____

Confirmation is not the end of the line. "I am confirmed now, so what else do I need to do?" The journey is only beginning. If you really take seriously your initiation, you will take an active role in the Church. You will realize more fully the importance of the other sacraments as well. You are now supposed to be different!

_____

_____

_____

CHRISTIAN INITIATION

# CONFIRMATION:
## *Believe and Celebrate*

These two pages are a chance for you to pull a few things together about your faith in the Holy Spirit and about the sacrament of Confirmation.

## SHARE

Choose one or more of the share activities below. Remember, each of them is for sharing with others.

1. *Spirit Signs:* Make a list of all the signs of the Holy Spirit you can find in your home, your school, your parish, or your neighborhood.

2. *Badge of Spirit Power:* In a small group, talk about how you would design a badge that you could wear to show the world that you believe in the Holy Spirit.

3. *Spirit-Filled People:* One of the best ways to learn about how Spirit-filled people are supposed to show their faith is to find living examples of other people who do. Find one person who you think is filled with the Holy Spirit and write a short story about him or her:

   ◆ How does this person treat others?
   ◆ What gives this person joy?
   ◆ What is different about this person?
   ◆ What makes **you** think this person is Spirit-filled?

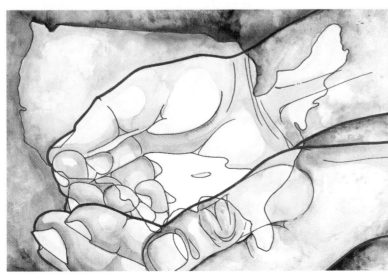

## ACTIVITIES

Pick one or more of the following actions to help you understand the power of the Spirit in your life.

1. Read about the Holy Spirit in the Bible. Try to find the passages yourself. Pick one passage and make a bumper sticker from a few key words in the passage.

2. Go to a place where you feel comfortable and safe—a place that is quiet and away from music and noise. In that space get really quiet. When you are quiet inside, say the words: "Come, Holy Spirit" over and over. Then be quiet and listen.

3. Seek out somebody who has recently gone through Christian Initiation or the sacrament of Confirmation. Ask him or her to tell you about the experience. Share your own feelings about what you are learning in your own search.

4. Spend five minutes a day reading the newspaper or a news magazine. Look for stories that cry out for the power of the Holy Spirit.

5. Talk with your family about what you are studying in *Christian Initiation*. Share your fears and doubts as well as your joys and hopes.

Pray

Take a few minutes to pray without words. In this space, draw, doodle, color, or scribble your prayer to the Holy Spirit. The only thing you cannot do is use words. Try it! It is not as hard as it sounds.

CHRISTIAN INITIATION

# LIVE WITH COURAGE

**The Spirit of Truth will bless you and give you courage to profess the true faith.**
*(Rite of Confirmation)*

# GIFTS AND TALENTS

## The two columns below are an opportunity for you to take an inventory of your gifts and talents.

Be sure to list at least five of your best qualities under the heading **GIFTS** and five special skills you possess under the heading **TALENTS**. (Don't be shy! A gift can be as simple as a ready smile, and a talent can be anything from a good fastball to accurate spelling.) Talk about how you use your gifts and your talents.

## GIFTS

_____

_____

_____

_____

## TALENTS

_____

_____

_____

_____

# Live MAKING FAITH WORK

The new hired hand sat cross-legged on a hillock overlooking the huge expanse of field. He had dreams of the field waving golden with wheat. He could almost smell the bread baking in the oven. But the request of the farmer was still ringing in his ears: "Get the south pasture ready for planting."

The young fellow really needed the job, so it never occurred to him to tell the farmer that he had no idea what that meant. Instead, he just said "okeydoke" and headed for the field. Now the field seemed to stretch on for miles. He was frustrated, afraid, and overwhelmed. At that moment, brain surgery seemed an easier task than preparing this huge field for planting.

He felt a hand on his shoulder. He turned his head and saw the warm smile of the farmer looking back at him. The smile spread to a grin, and the grin broke into a hearty laugh. "Son," said the farmer, "I admire your spirit. But it's my guess that you have a lot to learn."

"Yes, ma'am," answered the hired hand.

"You came out here so fast," the farmer said further, "I was certain you didn't have the slight-est idea where to start. Well, if you understand what you have to do, if you make the right start, and if you act with courage and responsibility, before too long that field will be planted, and we'll be waiting for the wheat to ripen."

## Powerful Gifts

Confirmed Christians have special gifts to help them follow Jesus. These gifts are much more powerful than a winning smile or a good fastball. They are gifts that make sure that the work Jesus began on earth goes on in the lives of those who follow Him.

> There are different gifts but the same Spirit; there are different ministries but the same Lord; there are different works but the same God who accomplishes all of them in everyone. To each person the manifestation of the Spirit is given for the common good. To one the Spirit gives wisdom in discourse, to another the power to express knowledge. Through the Spirit one receives faith; by the same Spirit another is given the gift of healing,

and still another miraculous powers. But it is one and the same Spirit who produces all these gifts, distributing them to each as he wills. (1 CORINTHIANS 12:4–11)

These gifts, called the "gifts of the Holy Spirit", are given to you at Confirmation. If you recall from the last chapter, they are each mentioned by the bishop in his prayer during the celebration of the sacrament. Take a look at what each gift means.

These gifts empower you with the wisdom, understanding, judgment, courage, and knowledge you need to be a person who lives for others. They also move you to reverence and to seek *communion* in wonder and awe with God who is Father, Son, and Holy Spirit. Take a look at what each gift means:

1. ***Wisdom*** is the gift that empowers you to know that there's more to life than meets the eye. It's the power to know what you could not know by self-analysis. This gift helps you live a truly human life.

2. ***Understanding*** is the gift that empowers you to recognize how God is active in your life.

3. ***Right Judgment*** is the gift that empowers you to discern the *meaning* of God's activity in your life and to choose the best way to respond to that activity.

4. ***Courage*** is the gift that empowers you to choose and act for someone or something beyond yourself.

5. ***Knowledge*** is the gift that empowers you to accept God's activity in your life and to get closer to God.

6. ***Reverence*** is the gift that empowers you to joyfully respect God and all God has given you.

7. ***Wonder and Awe*** together are a gift that empowers you

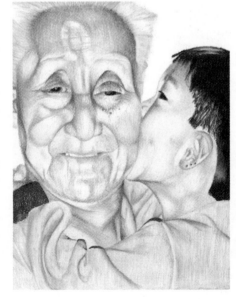

to admire and enjoy all God's gifts and to appreciate God's presence in all you do.

## Special Qualities

The tradition of the Church teaches that the Holy Spirit forms special qualities in those who have gone through Christian Initiation. These special qualities are sometimes called the "fruits of the Spirit." They are good habits or virtues. They are, in fact, qualities Christ himself possessed. People who work on these good habits will show Christ to others. They will be living their faith—their life in the Holy Spirit. Found in Scripture and in the tradition of the Church, there is usually a list of twelve of these special qualities. They are charity, joy, peace, patience, kindness, goodness, generosity, gentleness, faithfulness, self-control, modesty, and chastity. The gifts and qualities given to those who have been sealed with the Holy Spirit are not like the gifts of the fictional superheroes you see on television or read about in the comics. They really are much harder than that. All of the qualities you need to really follow Jesus demand, more than anything else, that you live with *courage.*

# MAKING FAITH WORK

## Questions

- Is there someone you admire who exhibits one or more of the gifts of the Holy Spirit or the fruits of the Holy Spirit? Share what you admire. Describe how this quality helps others.
- How do the people in your life value the gifts of the Holy Spirit? How do they value the fruits of the Holy Spirit?
- Which of the gifts of the Spirit are most important to you? Which do you feel are going to take the most courage for you to live out?

## Read and React

Read the paragraph below, then complete the chart to the best of your ability.

You are a gifted and talented person. You are beginning to learn how to develop and use your talents and gifts for the good of others. As a follower of Jesus, as somebody who has gone or is going through Christian Initiation, *who* you are is one way that the message of Jesus is supposed to get through to the world today.

On the chart below, write in each column simple ideas that you think will help you show the world that you have been confirmed in the Holy Spirit. Talk about how your gifts can help you be a better Catholic.

| I Can . . . | I Think I Could Be Good at . . . | I Really Like . . . | Someday I Would Like to . . . | Not Everyone Knows, But I'm . . . |
|---|---|---|---|---|
| | | | | |

# SUPPORT ONE ANOTHER

*Pray*

Every Christian gift is also a responsibility. You are called to share what you have received.

The Spirit is to be spent. Its message is for mission. Each gift of the Spirit, in its own unique way, helps you:

◆ Recognize God's presence in your life and in the world.
◆ Join your story to the story of Jesus and His Church.
◆ Witness to and share that Good News with others.

But none of this happens by magic. Confirmation doesn't change you overnight. You will have to grow into the gifts of the Spirit and learn how to use them best.

Luckily, the Church is here to help you. Remember, the Spirit and the gifts of the Spirit are given to a people (the Church), not just to individuals. Thank goodness for that. Through this Church, the gifts will always be available to you. They will bubble up at particular times and in particular ways in your life as you discover and learn to use the power of the Spirit to serve others.

You are at a time in your life when you are questioning, searching, and testing. You want to "own" your life, "own" your faith, and discover your own way. At the same time, you need support as you struggle and search. There is no one better to look to for that support than the Holy Spirit, whom Jesus calls both *Counselor* and *Guide*.

## A Challenging Friend

You have different kinds of friends. Some of your friends are easy-going and carefree and expect you to be the same. Some friends are good listeners and others are good talkers. You probably know so-called friends who want you to follow them into anger, rebellion, or even worse. You no doubt have at least one friend in your life who listens, counsels, comforts, but also *challenges* you. The Holy Spirit is that kind of friend.

When the Holy Spirit touched Peter and the other Apostles on Pentecost day, they were challenged to do something they never thought they could do. They stood up in front of thousands of people and told the story of Jesus and His

wonderful saving death and resurrection. They spoke so clearly that no matter what language their listeners spoke, they understood the words and asked the question: "What are we to do?"

Peter answered: "Repent and be baptized, every one of you, in the name of Jesus Christ for the forgiveness of your sins; and you will receive the gift of the Holy Spirit" (ACTS 2:38). That was the birthday of the Church. When you are baptized, that challenging Spirit is God's gift to you.

42

CHRISTIAN INITIATION

# Contact

The Holy Spirit is a Friend who wants you to be the best you can be. However, no friend can help, comfort, or even challenge you if you are not in contact. Don't leave all the contacting up to the Holy Spirit. There are many ways you can contact the Spirit. The steps below can help you contact your Challenging Friend in prayer.

*Call Out:* The Church uses many short prayers to call out to the Holy Spirit. Sometimes, you can use the simple phrase "Come, Holy Spirit." Sometimes a longer call is handy to know. "Come, Holy Spirit, fill my heart. Fire me up with your love." Send for your Spirit and they shall be created, and you will renew the face of the earth!

*Music and Atmosphere:* For centuries, people have used music, art, incense, candles, and the like to help them pray—to help them contact the Spirit. The music could be Church music, popular music, or instrumental music; anything that speaks best to your heart about love and peace. You know what songs call to you to be a more loving person and which songs tear you down. You also know what kind of atmosphere or art will help you get serious and pray.

*Readings from Scripture:* There is no better place to contact the Holy Spirit than God's Living Word in the Bible. Any story or prayer or song from the Bible helps in the contact, but some passages also teach about your Challenging Friend. The passages listed below are just such lessons:

- ◆ ISAIAH 42:1–4
- ◆ JOEL 2:1–2
- ◆ EPHESIANS 4:1–6
- ◆ MARK 1:9–11
- ◆ JOHN 7:37–39

*Quiet Time:* Sometimes the best way to contact the Holy Spirit is just to open your heart and listen. These are noisy times. Radios and televisions, stereos and video games, street noises and loud talking are part of your day. It is hard to concentrate or to listen in the midst of noise. A few moments of silence can be great contact times.

*A Litany Prayer:* For centuries, Christians have used simple litanies as powerful prayers. A simple sign of the cross followed by litany prayers like the one below can be great contact points, too:

O Holy Spirit, who at the first moment breathed life into the world:
**Come, renew us and the face of the earth.**

O Holy Spirit, who touched the lives and hearts of people throughout time, filling them with the power of God's love:
**Come, renew us and the face of the earth.**

O Holy Spirit, who came upon Jesus:
**Come, renew us and the face of the earth.**

O Holy Spirit, who descended upon the Apostles, giving them language of fire:
**Renew us and the face of the earth.**

O Holy Spirit, by whom we have been brought out of darkness into the light of Christ:
**Renew us and the face of the earth.**

O Holy Spirit, by whom the Church is guided and inspired:
**Renew us and the face of the earth.**

O Holy Spirit, who empowers us with seven-fold gifts that we may enjoy them and use them in service of others:
**Renew us and the face of the earth.**

# SUPPORT
## ONE ANOTHER

*A Summary Prayer:* Sometimes a simple formal prayer that sums up your thoughts and feelings can be a good contact point with the Holy Spirit.

> O Holy Spirit,
>
> Let your gifts give us power and courage. Let their light shine through our talents and our gifts. Brighten the lives of the people we serve. Guide us to the gifts we need. *Amen!*

If you roll all these steps together (call out, music and atmosphere, Scripture, quiet time, litany, and summing up), you and your friends will have your own special prayer service to help you contact the Holy Spirit. Try this prayer together. Be sure to add some personal touches.

## Questions

- ◆ What do you do when you face a challenge? Do you get frightened? Do you try to think things through? Do you try to get help? Describe how you act.
- ◆ Jesus said He came to bring Good News to the poor, freedom to prisoners, sight to blind people, and to proclaim a time of favor. How can you help in this mission?
- ◆ Have you ever prayed to the Holy Spirit? What was the occasion for your prayer?

## Read and React

The most basic gifts given to you in Baptism and Confirmation are the "big three": Faith, Hope, and Love. Read the three prayers below and add your own prayers of Faith, Hope, and Love.

### Faith:

O my God, I firmly believe that You are one God in Three Divine Persons: Father, Son, and Holy Spirit. I believe in Jesus Christ, Your Son. I believe all the truths which the Church believes and teaches, because You have revealed them. *Amen!*

_____

_____

_____

_____

### Hope:

O my God, I trust in Your goodness and promises. I hope to obtain forgiveness of my sins, the help of Your grace, and life everlasting through the merits of Jesus Christ, our Lord and Redeemer. *Amen!*

_____

_____

_____

_____

### Love:

O my God, I love You above all things because You are all-good and deserving of all my love. I love my neighbor as myself for love of You. I forgive those who have injured me, and I ask pardon of all whom I have injured. *Amen!*

_____

_____

_____

_____

# CONFIRMATION:
## *Live and Pray*

These two pages are a chance for you to get more in touch with how the sacrament of Confirmation helps you follow Jesus and contact God in prayer.

## SHARE

Choose one or more of the share activities below. Remember, each of these activities is for sharing with others.

1. *Spirit Search:* Look for signs of the *need* the world has for the Holy Spirit and for signs that the Spirit is *working* in the world. Here are some places to look:

   ◆ the daily newspaper or news magazines
   ◆ television news or magazine shows
   ◆ conversations with adult members of the parish
   ◆ your diocesan newspaper or parish bulletin

   Try to put what you discover in some written or graphic form so that it can easily be shared with others.

2. *Prayer Time:* Using the steps in the chapter, put together a prayer service inviting the Holy Spirit into your hearts. Don't be afraid to ask for help. Try to bring all your gifts and talents together in this service.

3. *At Your Service:* In small groups, plan a project to help people really in need. You don't have to do this all by yourself. You might participate in something that is already going on in your parish. As you make your plans, talk about which of the gifts of the Holy Spirit you will need to help you or how many of those special qualities, or virtues, you will need to complete your project.

## ACTIVITIES

Pick one or more of the following to help you live with courage and contact the Holy Spirit in prayer.

1. Say a morning prayer every day for the next week. (It is a good habit to always say a morning prayer.) In this prayer, offer your whole day to God and ask the Holy Spirit to help you live with courage.
2. Talk with your parents or other adults in your life about the Gifts of the Holy Spirit. Share with them what you are learning as you go through this time of Christian Initiation.
3. Make a personal motto for yourself. Keep the motto simple and to the point. Write out your motto and put it where it will challenge you to live with courage.
4. Go to Mass or some other worship service your parish offers on a day *other than* Sunday. You will find that this extra time of prayer and celebration can help you follow Jesus with great courage and love.

 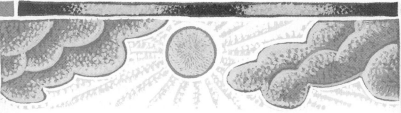

Catholic Christians have traditionally used what are called the "Works of Mercy" to remind them that they need to serve and help others. Use the two lists of works of mercy below to make a litany prayer that will challenge you to live in the power of the Holy Spirit. One list shows the corporal, or physical, works of mercy. The other shows more spiritual helps you can do for others.

_____

_____

_____

_____

_____

_____

_____

_____

### Corporal Works
1. Feed the hungry.
2. Give drink to the thirsty.
3. Clothe the naked.
4. Shelter the homeless.
5. Visit the sick.
6. Visit the imprisoned.
7. Bury the dead.

### Spiritual Works
1. Help the sinner.
2. Teach the ignorant.
3. Counsel the doubtful.
4. Comfort the sorrowing.
5. Bear wrongs patiently.
6. Forgive injuries.
7. Pray for the living and the dead.

CHAPTER

# GIVE
# THANKS

**We come to you with praise and thanksgiving.**
(*Eucharist*)

# THE THANK-YOU CARD

Every time somebody sends you a gift, you probably get nagged to write a thank-you card. Thank-you cards can be such a pain. It is a good bet that you have put off writing those cards for as long as possible.

Well, you have to write a thank-you card right here and right now. The card is right on this page, and the gift you have to be grateful for is the gift of your life. Use only the space on the card, but use as much of it as you can. Be as creative and clever as you can, but those are the only rules.

Oh, yes! You also have to be honest and sincere. Hurry up! Write your thank-you card.

*With Sincere Thanks*

# Believe

# GOODNESS GRACIOUS

The flames on the birthday candles danced and threw flickers of light across the dining room. The smell of chocolate cake filled the air. Balloons bumped against the ceiling, as if tickled by the chocolate cake's delicious smell. Four brightly wrapped packages lay on the table. Paper cups filled with sweet punch marked everyone's place.

At last, the family entered, leading Mom, who had a blindfold on. After she was led to her place and sat down, they took off the blindfold and shouted, "Happy birthday!"

"Goodness gracious!" said Mom as she opened her eyes, then quickly closed them as Steve snapped a flashbulb in her face. "Goodness gracious!"

Everyone clapped and crowded around Mom. Everyone wanted to be close to her on this special day. "Here," said Louise, waving a package sporting a colorful ribbon under Mom's nose. "This is from Dad. Open it first." Mom looked at Dad, and he smiled.

Mom unwrapped the package and found a photo album. Inside were pictures of Mom as a little girl, a teenager, and a bride. Mom started to sniffle a little, but then Josh pointed at the wedding picture and said, "Wow, Mom! You've got flowers in your hair, and Dad has a beard! You and Dad were hippies in the olden days!"

Mom and Dad laughed and shook their heads. "Goodness gracious no. We weren't hippies!" Mom said. Then, giving Dad a wink, she continued, "That's just the way everyone dressed back in the 'olden days.'"

"Open mine next," said Steve. Mom unwrapped Steve's package and found a homemade poster inside.

Mom read it aloud:

Bananas got peels. Peaches got fuzz.
But *I* got the best mom that ever was.

"Thank you, Steve," Mom said. "Goodness gracious, what a beautiful poster. I'm going to frame it and keep it always."

"Here, Mom," said Josh, handing her a heavy package. "This is for you."

It was a five-pound box of Mom's favorite candy. "Goodness gracious, Josh!" she exclaimed. "You must have spent all the money you saved from your paper route to afford this. Thank you, honey. Thank you so very much!"

"Okay, okay!" Louise piped up. "We've saved the best gift till last, *mine*. Open it."

When Mom opened the gift, all she could say was "Goodness gracious!" Louise's gift looked like a brightly colored, thick and heavy lump with a big safety pin sticking out

# GOODNESS GRACIOUS

of it. Mom took the lump from its box, scratched her head, and looked hopefully at her daughter.

"Goodness gracious!" Louise cried, "It's a corsage! You know, one of those fancy flowers. But you can keep this one forever. I made it out of play-clay. Put it on, Mom."

And that is exactly what Mom did.

Then, everyone sang "Happy Birthday." Mom blew out all the candles. Dad cut the cake. Louise dished ice cream. And the whole family ate and celebrated. They remembered the "olden days" and laughed at the photos in the album. They passed around the box of candy, and Mom told Josh to take an extra piece. Steve read his poem two or three times. And Mom pinned Louise's play-clay corsage over her heart, even though it kind of made her lean slightly to the left.

At bedtime, Mom asked everybody to join her in prayer. Everyone joined hands and bowed heads. "Goodness gracious . . ." Mom began.

## Gracious Goodness

Tiny flames from the lamps placed along the table danced and threw flickers of light across the Upper Room. The smell of roasting lamb filled the air. Large loaves of unleavened bread sat steaming on the table. A cup ready to be filled with the sweet wine of celebration marked each place. At last, Jesus and His friends entered and took their places at the table. Everything was ready for the Passover meal.

Jesus had wanted it this way. He wanted to share Passover with His friends. Passover was the feast where everyone remembered how God had saved the Jewish people from slavery in Egypt.

Jesus and His friends remembered the old stories of how God rescued their ancestors. Together, they shared the special foods and gave God thanks for rescuing them, too. By celebrating the Passover meal, they recognized that God's past saving activity on their behalf was present for them.

## God Remembers

The Passover meal celebrated "God remembering." And when God remembers, something happens even *now*, a saving action on behalf of God's people. As Jesus and His friends ate and drank, they understood that the Passover meal celebrated their salvation from slavery. They believed that the unleavened bread and the wine was a sharing "here and now" in "the sacrifice of Passover."

But then, just when the meal was almost over, Jesus did something different. Jesus did something brand new. Jesus did something very good and very gracious.

## This Is My Body

Jesus took some of the unleavened bread in His hands. He blessed the bread, broke it, gave it to His gathered friends, and said, "This is my body. Eat it to remember Me."

Then Jesus took a cup of wine, blessed it, and gave it to His friends.

"This is my blood. Drink it to remember Me," Jesus said. "Whenever you gather to break the bread and drink the cup to remember Me, I am with you."

## The Greatest Gift

The very next day, Jesus showed exactly how good and gracious His words and actions at the Last Supper actually were—how good and true they were. The very next day, Jesus' body was broken and His blood was poured out on the cross. Three days later, He rose to new life.

The bread broken at the Last Supper is Jesus' body broken for all. The wine shared at the Last Supper is Jesus' blood poured out for us. When we gather to share the bread and wine, then we are sharing in Jesus' death and resurrection.

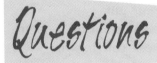
*Questions*

♦ What family celebration involving a meal do you most remember? Why? What was shared at the celebration? Food? Drink? What else?

♦ Why do so many of the most special celebrations involve a meal?

♦ What special meal were Jesus and His friends celebrating at the Last Supper? What *new* thing did Jesus do?

♦ What do you think Jesus meant when He told His friends to remember Him by breaking bread and drinking wine?

*Read and React*

Read the passage below. It is about the Holy Eucharist—the great prayer and action of giving thanks. Write what these words mean to you. Share what you have written. (You might want to read one of the following: MARK 14:22–25; MATTHEW 26:26–29; LUKE 22:15–20.)

For I received from the Lord what I also handed on to you, that the Lord Jesus, on the night He was handed over, took bread, and after He had given thanks, broke it and said, "This is My body that is for you. Do this in remembrance of Me." In the same way also the cup, after supper, saying, "This cup is the new covenant in My blood. Do this, as often as you drink it, in remembrance of Me. For as often as you eat this bread and drink the cup, you proclaim the death of the Lord until He comes." (1 CORINTHIANS 11:23–26)

_____

_____

_____

_____

_____

# REMEMBERING JESUS' GOOD GRACIOUSNESS

*Celebrate*

When Jesus told His friends to remember Him by breaking bread and drinking wine, He did not mean just to think about Him, like we sometimes think about the "olden days." In the Bible and in worship, *remembering* is a very special action. To remember means to make events from the past come alive *now*.

At the Last Supper, as Jesus and His friends ate and drank, they understood that the Passover meal they were sharing celebrated not only their ancestor's rescue from Egypt, but *their own* salvation from slavery. They believed that partaking of the unleavened bread and the wine was a sharing "here and now" in "the sacrifice of Passover."

When Jesus identified Himself with the bread and wine, He was identifying Himself as the *new* Passover sacrifice—proven the next day on the cross. Today, all who wish to share in that new Passover, "remember" Jesus by sharing the meal He left as a thanksgiving gift.

That is why, whenever you want to "remember" Jesus' gracious goodness, you do what Jesus asked all His followers to do. Gather, tell His story, break the bread, and share the cup. And believe, that when you do this, Jesus is with you *now*, in your gathering, in the priest who presides at the worship, in the Word of God that is proclaimed, and in the broken bread and cup. We call what we do the Eucharist or the Mass. The Eucharist is a powerful "remembering" of gracious goodness, and a wonderful celebration of *thankful* praise.

## The Mass—More than a Memory

It doesn't make any difference at all *where* the Eucharist is celebrated. It just makes all the difference in the world that people *do* celebrate Eucharist. For whenever you come together in thanks to remember Jesus in the gift of bread and wine, you are with Him as surely as if you were sitting in the Upper Room, as surely as if you were standing at the foot of His cross. The Eucharist makes the saving actions of Jesus *present tense*.

## Gather

The Eucharist begins with a gathering. No matter where people are from, no matter who they are, they all meet together as friends of Jesus.

52

CHRISTIAN INITIATION

Together, they mark themselves as baptized people: "In the name of the Father, and of the Son, and of the Holy Spirit. Amen."

## Share the Story

God's Word from the Bible—Old Testament, New Testament Letter, and Gospel—is proclaimed. The story of God's great love is read at every Mass. That story is not about "once upon a time." It is about right here, right now. Listen well to the story, so that it will become part of you and so that

you can join your story to that of Jesus. People *stand* for the Gospel to declare that this is Good News for Jesus' followers and Good News for everybody.

## Remember, Give Thanks, and Share

The Eucharist gathers all good things together. Every wonderful gift God has given is remembered. Every gift is offered and joined to Jesus' gift of Himself. The gifts that are offered are symbols of you.

The Eucharist also remembers the Last Supper. The good and gracious words and actions of Jesus are spoken and acted out again. You need to view these words and actions with the eyes of faith—from the perspective of Jesus' death and resurrection. That means believing that—by Jesus' word and action—the bread and wine are changed, re-shaped, and given new meaning and identity. They are more than food and drink. They are now the Body and Blood of Jesus, Lord and Savior, present with us to share, right here, right now. That's right! Really, honestly, and truly Jesus!

Together, everyone acclaims their faith in Jesus present by shouting or singing the Memorial Acclamation. Learn the following Memorial Acclamation by heart.

When we eat this bread and drink this cup, we proclaim Your death, Lord Jesus, until You come in glory.

Together, you share in Jesus' death and resurrection. Together, you eat the bread that is Jesus' Body for you and drink the wine that is

Jesus' Blood for you. Together, you give thanks for this wonderful meal that unites you to one another and to God.

The priest, deacon, or eucharistic minister presents the saving bread: "The Body of Christ."

**"Amen"** (We believe), is the faith-filled response.

The priest, deacon, or eucharistic minister presents the life-giving cup: "The Blood of Christ."

**"Amen"** (We believe), is the faith-filled response.

Communion is a sharing in the meal Jesus left us, the meal that is the new Passover, the meal that is Jesus Himself. Communion affirms the human need for food, for nurturing, for forgiveness, for one another, for God. And the Eucharist fulfills that need. More than that, it demands that you all be the Body of Christ for others.

## Promise

The Eucharist ends with a command: "Go. You are sent into the world!" The Eucharist ends with a blessing: "Go in peace." The Eucharist ends with a promise to obey the command and to share the blessing by serving others and welcoming them to the Lord's Table. You make your promise with gracious appreciation when you say, "Thanks be to God."

The Eucharist is a sacrament that celebrates how we are a people called to serve others. Both gathering to remember the story of God's love in Jesus, and breaking the bread and sharing in the

# REMEMBERING JESUS' GOOD GRACIOUSNESS

meal Jesus left as a gift and a command, commit you to give thanks to God and to give praise for the wondrous gift of Jesus.

The way you will offer fitting "thanks and praise" is by promising to serve one another and the world in the same way that Jesus served— and continues to serve—you!

## Questions

- ◆ What about Eucharist is like a family celebration?
- ◆ What is the name of the "family" with whom you celebrate Eucharist?
- ◆ Why does the Eucharist remember and celebrate both the Last Supper and Jesus' death and resurrection?

## Read and React

Read the following paragraph. Then, complete each of the items on the list. It will help you the very next time you go to Mass.

The Eucharist has much to give you. At the same time, the Eucharist asks much from you. If you really want to celebrate, you have to bring something to celebrate. Decide what you can bring to celebrate at Eucharist. Decide what you can do to make each moment of the Eucharist a good and gracious celebration for you and for the people with whom you worship.

1. When we **Gather** for Eucharist, I can:

2. To help **Share the Story of Jesus** at Eucharist, I will:

3. At Eucharist, I will **Remember**:

4. At Eucharist, I will **Give Thanks** for:

5. At Eucharist, I will **Share**:

6. Because of what I do at Eucharist, I **Promise**:

# EUCHARIST:
## *Believe and Celebrate*

These two pages are a chance for you to express your faith in the great prayer of thanksgiving—the Eucharist.

## SHARE

Choose one or more of the activities below. Remember, each of these activities is for sharing with others.

1. *The Best Gifts Ever:* Make a list of the top five gifts you have ever received. Be sure to note why you consider them the best ever. Answer these four questions for each gift you list.

   ◆ Was this gift a surprise?
   ◆ Was the gift something you really wanted?
   ◆ How did the giver know that you wanted this gift?
   ◆ What did the gift cost? (This is not about money. Add in time, energy, trouble and the like.)

2. *What's on the Menu?* For people throughout the world, food is more than just nourishment. Food is celebration. Describe your favorite meal. Why is it your favorite? What kinds of food do you consider important for celebrating? Describe the best meal you ever had. When you are through with this mouthwatering talk, draw a symbol for each of the words below:

   ◆ Hunger
   ◆ Nourishment
   ◆ Bread
   ◆ Life
   ◆ Fullness

   How do all these words and the symbols you made relate to the Eucharist?

3. *Next Sunday:* Prepare for next Sunday's Mass. Prepare as a class or as a small group. You might need a copy of the missalette used in your parish to help you.

   ◆ Find out what Sunday it is. (For example, it might be the First Sunday of Advent or the Twenty-third Sunday of the Year.)
   ◆ Read the opening prayer for this Sunday.
   ◆ Read through the three readings and talk about what you have read.
   ◆ Pray the responsory psalm together.

   After the Sunday Mass, share your experience. Did this preparation help you celebrate with your family and with your parish community? How did it help?

# ACTIVITIES

Pick one or more of the following actions to help you grow in your faith in the Eucharist.

1. Ask your parents or other family members if you can take turns leading a grace before meals. Try praying in your own words. Remember people outside the family who may be in need of food.

2. Practice three random acts of kindness. Promise to do something for a person in need. Be sure not to expect anything in return—not even a thank-you.

3. Take stock of your journey through this Christian Initiation program. Write a letter to a friend describing what you have learned and how you have changed.

4. Reach out and contact somebody who may not be feeling part of a community. A phone call, a card, a note, or a short visit can be a real Eucharistic moment filled with gracious goodness.

5. During the week, fill out a card listing the gifts you will be bringing to the Table of the Lord on Sunday. At the time the gifts are brought to the altar, read over your card. If you want to, put the card right in the offering basket.

## Pray

Together, share these thanksgiving words from Eucharistic Prayer Four:

Father in Heaven,
it is right that we should give You thanks and glory:
You alone are God, living and true.
Through all eternity You live in unapproachable light.
Source of life and goodness, You have created all things,
    to fill Your creatures with every blessing
    and lead all to the joyful vision of Your light.
Countless hosts of angels stand before You to do Your will;
    they look upon Your splendor
    and praise You, night and day.
United with them,
    and in the name of every creature under heaven,
    we, too, praise Your glory as we say:
Holy, holy, holy!

# CHAPTER *6* REMEMBER

**We proclaim Your death, Lord Jesus, until You come!**
(*Memorial Acclamation*)

# STORIES THAT LAST

**Everybody has stories** that come out every time friends or family gather. There was that time when Aunt Helen backed the car out of the garage, got out to close the garage door, then got into the back seat and started looking for the steering wheel. There was the Christmas when the new puppy arrived. Everybody remembers the time Mike played in the Little League World Series.

In the space below, tell one of your stories that lasts. Put in the details that make that story important to you. Be willing to share the story with others.

# Live MEMORIAL SACRIFICE

The Eucharist reminds you that—as thanks-filled sharers of the Body and Blood of Christ—you live out your thanks by becoming nourishment for others. Like nourishing eucharistic bread, which is broken and shared, you give thanks by committing yourself to be broken and shared with others, too. Like thirst-quenching eucharistic wine, which is poured out for others, you give thanks by committing yourself to be poured out for others. The two big words that Christians use to describe the Eucharist are *memorial sacrifice*. The words mean "remembering" and "giving of self for others." That is what Jesus did when He died for all. That is what you do when you participate at Mass.

## An Advanced Gratitude Attitude

Barney Casey was born November 25, 1870, as part of a large—*sixteen kids!*—farm family. He grew up working the soil, learning to tell time by the position of the sun, discovering how to smell coming weather, and developing a real feel and deep respect for the land and all things created. Even so, you couldn't keep Barney down on the farm.

When he was sixteen, Barney left home and went to the river town of Stillwater, Minnesota, where he got a job as a burler. That's someone who walks on water! Well, not really. A burler is someone who walks out on huge rafts of floating logs to make sure they keep moving down a river. When the logging season ended, Barney landed a job as a hod (brick) carrier by day and a part-time guard at the Stillwater State Prison by night. Barney made some interesting friends at the prison, including two members of the notorious Jesse James Gang, Jim and Cole Younger. Barney went on to become a trolley car conductor and then a motorman. He was searching for something, but just couldn't seem to find it.

## Answering a Call

Finally, at the ripe old age of twenty-one, Barney entered the seminary to study for the priesthood. Unfortunately, he was no whiz kid. The courses were difficult and in German—no easy language for a farm boy from an Irish family. After five years of study, Barney's professors told him that he really wasn't qualified to be a priest and sent him home.

Barney was really hurting and confused. He needed some guidance, some help, a clear voice giving him direction. He got it. One evening, while he was praying, Barney felt he heard the words, "Go to Detroit." Not what you'd call your great revelation, right? But Barney paid attention. Detroit was where the Capuchin Franciscans were located. On Christmas Eve, 1896, Barney entered the Capuchin Monastery in Detroit. He didn't know it then, but he'd found a new home. Three weeks later, he got a new name. Barney Casey became Solanus Casey, Capuchin.

# MEMORIAL SACRIFICE

## The Doorman

The studies for the priesthood at the monastery weren't any easier for Barney—now Brother Solanus. Once again, the courses were in German, and Solanus had a lot of trouble with them. It took him eight years, but finally, Solanus was ordained a priest. He could preside at Mass, but he was not allowed to preach or hear confessions (celebrate the sacrament of Reconciliation with penitents). Solanus was sent to New York, where, not knowing exactly what to do with a priest who couldn't preach or hear confessions, the superior made him the monastery's doorman (or porter, as the Capuchins call it).

Now, a person might think that getting ordained just to answer the door would be quite a comedown, right? Not Father Solanus. He really believed in the words from HEBREWS: "Do not neglect to show hospitality, for by doing so, some have entertained angels without knowing it."

Well, it wasn't long before people started coming to the monastery door just to talk to Solanus—to hear his simple greeting, to ask his advice, or to seek his help. Solanus never sent anyone away unsatisfied. He welcomed strangers as long-lost guests. He encouraged those who sought guidance not to worry but to have confidence in God. He urged those who were hungry for meaning to come back to the Eucharist and be satisfied. He reminded those who asked for assistance or healing to give thanks *ahead of time* for the help God would surely send.

In 1924, after serving twenty years in New York, Solanus returned to St. Bonaventure Friary in Detroit. There, he took up duties as doorman again. And once again, people flocked to him.

## Be the Miracle

Solanus said that people's "greatness lies in being faithful to the present moment." He lived that out by always being available to those who were poor, or sick, or seeking deeper faith. He made a special effort to connect with each person he met. In turn, he invited every person he met to connect with God.

Pretty soon, people were relating some amazing things about Solanus. The sick who had come to see him reported cures. The poor he had touched talked of favors granted. The faithless he had counseled returned to faith. Some said that Solanus was a miracle worker. And more and more people came knocking on the friary door.

Solanus didn't claim to be a miracle worker. He recognized that miracles are signs of faith, and that faith can work miracles. So he urged others to have faith, to be confident. He encouraged people not to ". . . pray for tasks equal to your powers; pray for powers equal to your tasks—then the doing of your work shall be no miracle, but you shall be a miracle."

## A Eucharistic Life

Solanus' life proved that you could be a person of thanks who nourished others on a log-raft, in a prison cell, at the controls of a streetcar, or the

# MEMORIAL SACRIFICE

door of a friary. He knew that being a thankful person wasn't always easy. But he also knew that it was the most exciting way to live.

After fifty-three years of priesthood and door-opening, on July 31, 1957, Solanus (Barney) Casey died. Since his death, many people have called him a saint. In fact, the Catholic Church is looking into canonizing him. Solanus never once passed up the opportunity to act with gratefulness and generosity. And he always gave thanks for God's nourishing generosity—in advance.

## Questions

♦ How did Father Solanus give thanks and nourish others?
♦ What do you think having a "gratitude attitude" means?
♦ What do the followers of Jesus remember at Mass?
♦ How would you describe the words "Memorial Sacrifice"?

## Read and React

Read the paragraph below. Describe how you intend to make the Mass a more important part of your life. Write out your own "advanced gratitude attitude."

The [newly baptized] devoted themselves to the teaching of the Apostles and to the communal life, to the breaking of the bread and to the prayers. Awe came upon everyone, and many wonders and signs were done through the Apostles. All who believed were together and had all things in common; they would sell their property and possessions and divide them among all according to each one's need. Every day they devoted themselves to meeting together in the temple area and to breaking bread in their homes. They ate their meals with joy and sincerity of heart, praising God and enjoying favor with all the people. And every day the Lord added to their number those who were being saved. (ACTS 2:42–47)

**My Gratitude Attitude**

# DO THIS IN MEMORY OF ME

*Pray*

Christians begin each week with a celebration. They gather together as a people who are wondrously related to God and one another. The Sunday gathering shapes and affirms the belief that welcome, thanks, service, and caring are the ingredients of relationship and the meaning of the Christian's mission in the world.

You are part of a people who remember and make Eucharist—who are gracious and thankful. You are one of the eucharistic people. From the soles of your feet to the top of your head, you know that, as a Catholic, the Mass is your chance to obey the request Jesus made of you on the night before He died, "Do this in memory of Me."

It will be most helpful if you understand just what happens in this great prayer.

## Gather Together

Christians come together to celebrate Eucharist. Mass is not a private event. Christians believe that Christ himself is present as they gather. The priest or bishop who presides at the Eucharist is a reminder that Christ is present. At Mass, everybody has a role to play—presiding and offering, reading, singing, responding, bringing up gifts, giving Communion. Everybody can also say "Amen!" to show agreement with everything that is remembered and celebrated.

## Liturgy of the Word

At every Eucharistic celebration, the Scripture is read. There are always at least two readings. On Sunday, there are three—one from the Hebrew Scriptures, another from the writings of the Apostles, and a reading from one of the four Gospels.

Christians believe that God is present in the Word. When the Word is proclaimed before the people, it is as alive and fresh as when it was first spoken or written thousands of years ago. Every Sunday, there is also a homily (a fancy word for a brief sermon). The homily is a personal witness

to the gathered people to accept God's Word with an open heart and an open mind and to act on that Word.

After the reading and witnessing, the whole gathered community offers special prayers for the community and its needs.

## Giving Gifts

Now it is time to set the table for the Meal of Meals. The bread and wine are brought to the altar. Sometimes they are brought from the center of the Church. The bread and the wine (which will soon be the Body and Blood of Christ) bundle up every gift you and those with you have to offer. It is a wonderful gesture of sacrifice. "Here, take what we grow and what we make! Make these gifts wonderful!"

There is a long tradition of bringing other gifts to the altar. Ages ago, people brought food for the clergy, clothing for the poor, and money for the needs of the community. At most Sunday Masses there is a collection of money. Often the basket is brought right to the altar with the bread and the wine.

## The Prayer of Remembering

Now comes the most important moment of the celebration. It is the time of the great Prayer of Remembering. It is the heart of the celebration. You might not know, but this prayer has several parts.

1. **The Preface:** In this part, the people give thanks to the Father, through Jesus in the Holy Spirit, for every good gift. It ends with the words "Holy, holy, holy . . ."

2. **Come, Holy Spirit:** The community asks the Father to send the Holy Spirit on the bread and the wine so that they might become the Body and Blood of Jesus.

3. **The Words of Jesus:** Then the celebrant repeats the words and actions of Jesus at the Last Supper. These words make Jesus present under the forms of bread and wine.

4. **The Remembering:** The part of the prayer that follows remembers the suffering, death, resurrection, and the coming again of Jesus.

5. **The Petitions:** The community then asks God to remember the whole Church, all the members, and their needs.

6. **The Final Praise:** Finally the prayer breaks out with joy and proclaims: "Through Him, with Him, in Him, in the union of the Holy Spirit, all glory and praise are Yours, Almighty Father, now and forever!" *AMEN!!!*

# DO THIS
# IN MEMORY OF ME

## Communion

The community then shares the prayer that was a special gift from Jesus to His friends—the Lord's Prayer. After an exchange of a greeting of peace, the followers of Jesus come forward to receive the host and the cup. Together, all are fed, nourished, challenged, and encouraged by the Body and Blood of Christ.

## Questions

- ◆ How do you act when you are at the Eucharist? Are you bored? distracted? edgy?
- ◆ What changes can you make in yourself so that you are more present when you are at Mass?
- ◆ How does your parish community try to reach out to you and your needs at Mass?

## Read and React

The material below was written by Saint Justin around the year AD 155. Read it carefully and write down your reactions.

On the day we call the day of the sun, all who dwell in the city or country gather in the same place. The memories of the Apostles and the writings of the Prophets are read, as much as time permits.

When the reading is finshed, he who presides over those gathered challenges the people to imitate these beautiful things. Then, we all rise together and offer prayers for ourselves and for all others, wherever they may be, so that we may be found just by our life and actions, and faithful to the Commandments.

When the prayers are finished, we exchange the kiss. Then someone brings bread and a cup of water and wine mixed together to him who presides over the brothers and sisters. He takes them and offers praise and glory to the Father of the universe, through the name of the Son and of the Holy Spirit and for a considerable time he gives thanks that we have been judged worthy of these gifts.

When he has finished the prayers and thanksgivings, all present give voice to an acclamation by saying: "Amen!" When thanks has been given and the people have responded, those we call deacons give to those present the Eucharistic bread and take it to those who are absent.

(*Saint Justin's Apology*, 1:65–67)

# EUCHARIST:
## *Live and Pray*

These two pages are a chance for you to choose how you will live the Eucharist every day and how you will pray the Eucharist with all your heart.

## SHARE

Choose one or more of the share activities below. Remember, each of these activities is for sharing with others.

1. *Nourishing Thanks:* Create a "Nourishing Thanks" box for your family. Cover a shoe box and its lid with plain paper. Make sure you can lift off the lid. Then, cut a slit in it. Print the phrase *nourishing thanks* on the box. Decorate it any way you choose. Place slips of paper and a pencil near the box. Tell family members that they can either write a prayer or ask for prayers simply by placing them in the box. Plan to open the box at a specific mealtime each week— Saturday supper perhaps. Share the prayers.

2. *We Serve:* Select a person or group you could help nourish. Is there a family in the parish that needs groceries, someone you know who needs a friend, a friend who is lonesome, a homeless shelter that needs someone to serve dinner? Together or in a small group, select a way that you can serve and become nourishment to others.

3. *Remember Time:* Search your memory for moments that made a difference. Make a list of strong memories you have that somehow caused you to be changed. Maybe taking too many chances on skates or on your bike caused you to break an arm. Maybe the death of your old yellow dog got you to think about what it means to live and be loyal. Write down some of your memories. Talk about them and share how these moments can help you understand and live the Eucharist.

## ACTIVITIES

Select one or more of the following actions to help you develop an advanced gratitude attitude.

1. Go to Mass with a friend. Go on your own without parents or other adults. After the Mass is over, talk about what you shared.

2. Find more saints. Look for stories of famous (or not-so-famous) followers of Jesus. See if you can find in their stories some signs of their gratitude and their love for the Eucharist.

3. Volunteer to help prepare a meal, serve a meal, or (ouch!) clean up after a meal. Don't do this on a day you are supposed to do it. How does this help you understand the Eucharist?

4. Read the story of the Last Supper in the Gospel of JOHN. (You can find it if you try!) John does not mention the Eucharist, but try to find examples of the gratitude attitude in what you read.

5. Make yourself a reminder (poster, sign for your bike, bumper sticker, stick-on note for your mirror) that will help you keep the Eucharist in mind.

6. Next time you are at Mass, try to notice all the parts that you learned about in this chapter.

First, share at least two of the readings listed below. Then make up a litany prayer to help you remember how important it is to live the Eucharist and to love the Eucharist. Write a response in the space below.

### Readings:

◆ PSALM 104:10–15
(Thanks to a generous God)

◆ 1 CORINTHIANS 10:16–17
(One bread, one Body)

◆ JOHN 6:28–35
(The Bread of Life)

◆ LUKE 24: 13–35
(In the breaking of the bread)

CHAPTER 7

# ALWAYS
# COME
# HOME

**May God give you pardon and peace!**
(*Rite of Penance*)

# WORDS OF A FEATHER

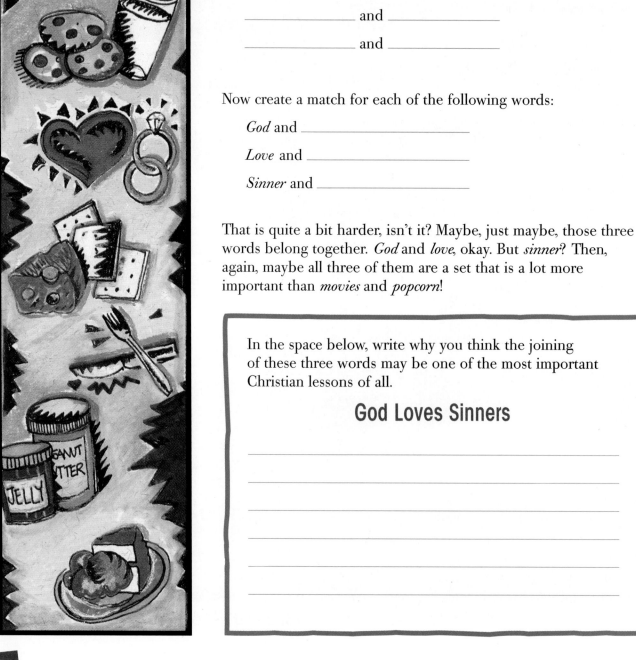

Some words just seem to be meant for each other.

For example: ***milk and cookies, burger and fries, love and marriage, peanut butter and jelly***.

Jot down a few more pairs of words that go together.

_____ and _____

_____ and _____

_____ and _____

Now create a match for each of the following words:

*God* and _____

*Love* and _____

*Sinner* and _____

That is quite a bit harder, isn't it? Maybe, just maybe, those three words belong together. *God* and *love*, okay. But *sinner*? Then, again, maybe all three of them are a set that is a lot more important than *movies* and *popcorn*!

In the space below, write why you think the joining of these three words may be one of the most important Christian lessons of all.

## God Loves Sinners

_____

_____

_____

_____

_____

_____

# THE PRODIGAL

It was just another dawn, and the arthritic old farmer followed his simple morning routine. His hired hands shook their heads and mumbled to one another as they watched him shuffle down the farmyard drive and out onto the road. When he reached the byway, as he had done on so many mornings, the old man looked long and hard toward the distant hills. He lifted his hand to his brow to shade his eyes from the early sun.

Cresting the jagged hills, a bedraggled figure was approaching. He wore no cloak, no sandals, no ring as would be the signs of a person of any rank. None of that would have been noticed by the old man, whose eyes were not what they once were. And yet, the old man knew the figure at once. He turned to his hired hands and shouted, "My son! My son is come home! Let's celebrate!"

To finish the story, read LUKE 15:11–31. Sum it up in your own words below.

_____

_____

_____

_____

## A Father's Love

The father in the story of the Prodigal Son is forgiveness in the flesh. He doesn't wait for repentance; he seeks it out. He doesn't demand punishment but is ready to forgive and forget. He refuses to see darkness, sin, and death as the conclusion to his story, but rejoices in light, forgiveness, and life. He welcomes his wasteful son with open arms, drowning his words of confession in celebration.

He coaxes his angry elder son with an open heart, urging him to share in his kindness and generosity. He refuses to mourn, but rushes to throw a party for the lost that was found, for the dead that has come back to life. He is the forgiving, reconciling father, who shows us that *God* and *love* and *sinner* are words that really do belong together and will for all time.

This is the father whose great love comes to mind every time the followers of Jesus celebrate the sacrament of Reconciliation.

## The Homecoming Sacrament

Jesus' parable of the prodigal son and his generous father is unbelievably good news. Jesus proclaims the bountiful forgiveness of God and calls for reconciliation—no matter what. Sin will be forgiven. All you have to do is admit you did wrong and *come home*.

The Church celebrates the heart's movement toward God and toward others in the sacrament of Reconciliation. The celebration of the sacrament of Reconciliation is grander than any fatted-calf feast. It is the great homecoming of wayward Christians. In the sacrament, what was lost is found, what was dead comes to life again.

In the sacrament, the faith community accepts all weary attempts at expressing and asking for forgiveness (like that of the younger son). It also teaches every follower of Jesus to correct his or her petty and stingy holding back of forgiveness (like that of the elder son).

In this great sacrament, God, the giving Father, bends to the sinner with words of welcome. God sees contrite hearts and anticipates struggling words of sorrow. Through the ministry of the Church and the hands and words of the priest, sin is forgiven, and the sinner can celebrate a homecoming so grand as to make the sinner feel as if he or she had never left.

## Reconciliation and Life

Saint Paul reminds those who follow Jesus that reconciliation is a ministry all share:

> Anyone who is in Christ is a brand new creation. All the old ways are done. Now all things are new! All things are new because we are reconciled to God in Jesus Christ. Even more, God has given us the ministry of reconciliation. I mean that God, in Christ, is reconciling the world to Himself. God does not count sins against us. Instead, God has given us the message of reconciliation.
>
> (2 CORINTHIANS 5:17–19)

## Act Forgiven

The sacrament of Reconciliation is not one of the sacraments of Initiation. But, by your baptism and confirmation and your reception of Holy Eucharist, you are forgiven and reconciled. The way we live should show that. Regular and frequent reception of the sacrament of Reconciliation is one way of acting forgiven, of regularly turning away from selfishness, coming back to God's love, and helping other people do the same.

# Believe
# THE PRODIGAL

Of course, another way to act forgiven is to be willing to forgive. Followers of Jesus are bold enough to pray, "forgive us as we forgive." To help you be more forgiving, try to develop three habits:

1. *Be understanding.* People with the habit of understanding know that there are always two sides to every story.
2. *Be kind.* People with the attitude of kindness are able to keep from judging others and to treat them with dignity and respect.
3. *Have mercy.* People with the habit of mercy have healing hearts. They are not interested in revenge.

## Questions

◆ Have you ever felt like you *really* needed to be forgiven? What did it feel like? What did you do?
◆ How good are you at forgiving others? Do you hold a grudge? What does holding a grudge say about you?
◆ Why is the homecoming sacrament such a great gift for the followers of Jesus?

## Read and React

Read the paragraph below. Then, write your own reactions to it. What can you do to remember the lesson of this paragraph?

The greatest enemy of sin is not law enforcement, regulations, prison, punishment, vengeance, penalties, or rejection. The biggest enemy of sin is *forgiveness.* Jesus was a victim of sin. Sin, selfishness, hate, jealousy, envy, and a whole list of other offenses had nailed Him to a cross. Petty and hateful people stood around the cross and teased Jesus. The civilized world was crumbling around them, and they had time to poke fun at a dying political criminal. "Father, forgive them," Jesus said. Nobody was asking for forgiveness. Nobody was real anxious to give up sinful ways. Yet, without any request at all, Jesus handed out forgiveness.

_____

_____

_____

_____

# WORDS
# TO LIVE BY

*live*

Forgiveness and reconciliation. The whole of Christianity revolves around these words. The Christian family survives because of them. The words sustain people. They can't be categorized or understood in any logical way. They are medicine, restoring all those led by sin and failure to love and new hope. They restore the future and banish fear. They put the family back together.

## Faith in Action

One of the big misunderstandings about this sacrament is expressed in the sentiment: "If God is so forgiving, why can't I just tell God I am sorry and be forgiven in my heart? Why do I have to tell a priest or go to a penance service?"

The answer is very simple. If you ran away from home like the Prodigal Son did, you could not get home "in your heart." To show that you wanted to be back with your family, you would have to pick yourself up and head home—*in person*. The sacrament of Reconciliation is your chance to come home *in person*. Once you get home, you *will* be forgiven and welcomed back.

The sacrament of Reconciliation is faith in action! The community believes in the gift of forgiveness and does something about it. It might help if you take a quick look at just how a communal celebration of the homecoming sacrament works:

1. *Greeting:* With a song of praise, people gather together. The priest greets everyone: "Grace, mercy, and peace be with you." This welcome is a reminder that God's grace and love are already present, have been present, and have touched sinners before the first thoughts of sorrow and the first desires to come home.

2. *Celebration of the Word:* God's Word is proclaimed. That loving Word urges all to examine their consciences and be sorry for their sins. It invites everyone to look forward in expectation to a life renewed.

3. *Confession of Sins:* Each person confesses his or her sins to the priest. Confession is the way to respond to God's love. It is an act of conversion, or change of heart. Confession is the way to face up to humanness and offer it to God. This is something pretty amazing. In the sacrament of Reconciliation, you can offer yourself to God even at your worst! All you

need do is admit you are wrong and be willing to change.

4.  *Absolution:* The priest gives each person absolution, or sacramental forgiveness. Just as God received Jesus' offering of Himself "for the forgiveness of sins," so God receives your offering for forgiveness. In God's name, the priest gives this forgiveness. Here are the words he uses:

> God, the Father of mercies,
> through the death and resurrection
>    of His Son
> has reconciled the world to Himself
> and sent the Holy Spirit among us
> for the forgiveness of sins;
> through the ministry of the Church
> may God give you pardon and peace,
> and I absolve you from your sins
> in the name of the Father, and of the
>    Son,
> and of the Holy Spirit.
> *Amen!*          (*Rite of Penance*, 55)

5.  *A Penance:* The priest will give each person a prayer to say or a good deed to do. This is called "the penance." Saying the prayer or doing the deed shows you accept the forgiveness you have received.

6.  *Praise for God's Mercy:* Everyone then offers God praise and thanks. Celebrating the sacrament of reconciliation has turned people around. The inward look of selfishness is now turned outward to the God who loves sinners. A sinful people have become thankful. Everybody is back facing the right direction.

7.  *Dismissal:* This celebration has given people a share in the same peace the risen Lord gave His Apostles. The priest dismisses people to do what peacemakers do—forgive others.

## How Many Times?

Peter was a burly fisherman. He knew limits. He knew how many fish his net could hold. He knew the shoreline of the lake. He knew the changing times of sunrise and sunset, and where the fish would be at precisely those moments. Peter knew his boat, too. He knew the strength of the mast and the power of the sail. Peter also knew his own limitations. He chose to ignore them when he was swept away by the sudden storms of temper he experienced on occasion. But all in all, Peter knew the limits.

It made sense for Peter to check with Jesus to find out the limits of forgiveness. Now, Peter had been paying attention to the message. He was sure that the Master was going to demand a lot of his followers as far as forgiveness was concerned. So, before Peter popped the forgiveness question, he decided in advance on what would be a generous serving of generosity.

# WORDS TO LIVE BY

Peter cleared his throat and asked, "How many times should I forgive my neighbor? Seven times?" Peter looked around the group. He expected to see some eyebrows raised quite high at so lavish a show of mercy. He expected his fellow disciples to nod approval at Peter's big heart.

He was still looking for approval when he heard the Master's answer. "No, Peter," Jesus corrected, "not seven times, but seventy times seven times."

"Wait a minute!" Peter thought to himself. He knew that figure of speech. He used it himself to describe a catch of fish. ("We caught a hundred times a hundred fish.") It meant the catch was "without limit." Jesus was telling His disciples that they were supposed to forgive *without limit*. For a moment, Peter was not sure his heart was that big.

## A Big Heart

One of the biggest lessons of the sacrament of Reconciliation is the lesson that the forgiveness you receive is a gift to be passed on to others. There is not much room in the Christian heart for hate or hurt. But your heart needs to be big enough to say, "I forgive you!"

## Questions

◆ When was the last time you asked for forgiveness? What were the results?

◆ Who is your personal living model of a forgiving person? Who demonstrates best for you understanding and mercy?

◆ How would you like to be described at your funeral? (Seem silly? Well, the answer most people give is that they had "a big heart.") A Christian's big heart is rooted in reconciliation and forgiveness.

## Read and React

Read the passage below. It is from the Gospel of JOHN. Then, write your reactions to the reading. Try to imagine how the Apostles felt at the moment Jesus breathed on them.

On the evening of that first day of the week, even though the disciples had locked the doors of the place where they were, Jesus came and stood before them. "Peace be with you," He said. When He had said this, He showed them His hands and His side. At the sight of the Lord the disciples rejoiced. "Peace be with you," He said again.

"As the Father has sent Me, so I send you." Then He breathed on them and said:

"Receive the Holy Spirit. If you forgive sins, they are forgiven. If you hold them bound they are held bound." (JOHN 20:19–23)

# RECONCILIATION:
## *Believe and Live*

These two pages are a chance for you to think over the importance of the sacrament of Reconciliation and to discover how to live what you believe.

## SHARE

Choose one or more of the share activities below. Remember, each of these activities is for sharing with others.

1. *Media Watch:* During the week, monitor television, newspapers, popular music, and other media. Try to discover both the need for and the act of forgiveness. Try to make a specific list of instances. Share what you have discovered. See if you can tell from what you discover just how much society values forgiveness. It will also be interesting to find out how many examples of *revenge* you can find. How is revenge the enemy of forgiveness?

2. *Forgiveness Roadblocks:* Forgiving and asking for forgiveness are not easy tasks. The elder brother in the story of the Prodigal Son was kept from forgiving by his jealousy. Take one day out of your life and make an inventory of the roadblocks you find in your own life that keep you both from forgiving others and from asking for forgiveness. For each roadblock ask the following questions:
   ◆ How did this roadblock get into my life?
   ◆ Why is this a forgiveness roadblock?
   ◆ What can I do to get this roadblock out of my life?

3. *Bible Study:* Read each of the Scripture passages listed below. After each reading, talk over or write down how this passage can help you be more forgiving.
   ◆ LUKE 19:1–10 (a little man up a tree)
   ◆ LUKE 6:27–38 (a tall forgiveness order)
   ◆ ROMANS 12:9–21 (peace)
   ◆ COLOSSIANS 3:12–17 (love)

# ACTIVITIES

Pick one or more of the following to help you develop a habit of forgiveness.

1. Before you go to Mass with your family the next time, see to it that everyone has forgiven one another for the hurts (big and little) that have happened during the week. Take time to say "I'm sorry" and "I forgive."

2. Make a few forgiveness reminders and place them around where you will run into them later. This can be done as simply as writing $70 \times 7$ on a few self-adhesive notes and putting them where they will do you some good.

3. Make a visit to the Blessed Sacrament. In the quiet of the church, ask Jesus to help you develop the habit of being forgiven and of forgiving. Ask for help to make regular use of the sacrament of Reconciliation.

## Pray

The list below will help you prepare for the sacrament of Reconciliation.

1. *Music:* Choose a hymn or a quiet piece of music to set a mood for preparation.

2. *The Scripture:* Read at least two of the following passages:
   ◆ ISAIAH 1:10–18 (turn from selfishness)
   ◆ PSALM 51 (have mercy)
   ◆ ROMANS 13:8–14 (turn to the light)
   ◆ MATTHEW 9:9–13 (Jesus calls sinners back)

3. *Litany:* Pray a litany prayer with the response, "Lord, have mercy." The following will help. But you can add petitions of your own.
   ◆ In sorrow for our selfishness, we pray:
   ◆ Regretting that we hurt others, we pray:
   ◆ With confidence in Your love, we pray:

4. *A Sign:* Form a circle and join hands. Send a signal of forgiveness by squeezing the hand of the person next to you. The sign will pass all around the circle.

5. *Praise:* Together share the following prayer:

   Loving God, You seek us out. You pardon us and welcome us home. Thank You for helping us grow and change. Thank You for supporting us when we fail. Thank You for forgiving us and calling us to forgive others in the name of Jesus Christ our Lord. *Amen!*

CHRISTIAN INITIATION

# A Little Catechism

## Why a Catechism?

Have you ever gone on a journey with your family to a new and different country or city? How did you find your way? How did you know what to do, what to see, where to stay and eat? Did you have friends or relatives there who served as your hosts and guides? If not, did you purchase a quality guidebook to help you find your way around?

A good guidebook helps travelers lay out the stages of a journey, stay true to their bearings, prevent them from getting turned around, and make it safely to their destination. It points out hazards and roadblocks, but it also draws attention to fascinating features. Even the best guidebook doesn't tell travelers everything crucial about their journey and destination. However, every quality guidebook always includes important and interesting information that helps make the journey enjoyable and exciting.

## The Church's Guidebook

A catechism is something like a quality guidebook—a guidebook for the faith journey. A catechism doesn't show you everything about faith or what it means to be a Catholic Christian. It doesn't explain every line of Scripture. It can't wrap up what it means to be a person of faith in a neat package. It doesn't teach the whole of Church tradition. It can't force you to worship, ensure that you follow Jesus, or fill you with prayer. In other words, a catechism can't *make* you Catholics. Knowing even the best catechism by heart, won't guarantee that you will reach your destination without some detours along the way.

## A Brief Guide

However, a catechism can guide you through the many interesting and important avenues of faith. Like a guidebook to a strange and wonderful city, it draws attention to issues of interest and details of delight. It can make you curious to know more, discover more, and to continue your faith journey.

Use the little catechism on the following pages as a guide to discover

◆ what Catholic Christians believe
◆ how faith is celebrated and shaped
◆ how faith is lived
◆ how Christians support faith in prayer

# WOUNDED DUCK

Melody Morgan was born to run—but never gracefully. Her gangly arms ended in stubby hands that constantly flapped as she moved. Her running stride was not much better. She ran with a rapid waddle, her legs and feet splaying out from side to side. Even after coaching helped Melody with her starts and breathing, her running style remained unchanged. No wonder, then, in high school, the girls in varsity track gave her the cruel nickname "Wounded Duck."

## A Champion

In her senior year, Melody led her college team to the women's national track and field championships. By then, every time Melody ran, excited fans stomped their feet and chanted together, "Woun-ded Duck! Woun-ded Duck!" That chorus seemed to set the pace for Melody's running. As each race neared the finish line, the chanting of her fans increased in rhythm and speed, and Melody's pace quickened in response. By the end of the meet, Melody had been the first to reach the finish line seven times.

After college, Melody went into coaching high school. The nickname "Wounded Duck" stuck with her even as a coach. She inspired many young women to have faith in themselves and to do their best, but she never taught anyone to run in her strange style. Finally, after years of coaching, Melody

revealed in an interview for the high school newspaper the reason she ran the way she did.

## Solid Faith

Melody Morgan was partially blind. She saw double—especially when she was running. Her poor vision was aggravated by a fluid imbalance in her inner ear. Neither glasses nor surgery could help her. Melody had adopted the running style which had earned her that cruel nickname just so she wouldn't fall down.

When the interviewer for the paper asked her if it was difficult for her to run, Melody responded, "Yes and no." All of the races she ever ran began in a sort of obscure dimness. She could never see clearly quite where she stood or where the finish line really was. She had to work hard to focus, maintain concentration, and keep from falling. "I never could actually see where I was going," Melody said, "but I always believed I could get there. Something inside me always drove me on. As the race went, I'd stop running by sight, and the next thing I'd know, I'd won."

"Did it bother you being called *Wounded Duck*?" the interviewer asked Melody.

"Well, it isn't a very flattering name, but no—it never did," she chuckled. "In fact, if it hadn't been for people's faith in me, their chanting my name, their pacing my course, I don't think I ever would have become a champion." Melody Morgan—*Wounded Duck*—had faith enough to fly.

*Believe*

# WE BELIEVE

What is it that Catholic Christians believe? What is "the faith"? Here is a summary of what Catholic Christians cherish and hold as precious:

1. **We believe in a God whom we call Father, a generous, loving parent, who created us and all things.**

   ◆ We affirm that all things belong to God, not to us.

   ◆ We say that there is far more here than we can understand, own, or control.

   ◆ We declare that we are not the center of the universe, that there is One bigger and grander who made us and loves us beyond imagining.

2. **We believe in Jesus Christ, God's only Son, our Lord, who became a human being so that we might know God's love in the flesh.**

   ◆ We profess that God loved us so much, God became a human being to show us who God is—extravagant, forgiving, compassionate, and saving Love.

   ◆ We declare that Jesus went so far as to suggest that in His name we could become God's children.

   ◆ We recognize that Jesus challenges us to live as God's own children in joyful, thankful, and compassionate concern for others.

3. **We believe that Jesus Christ lived among us, suffered for our sakes, was crucified, died and was buried, descended into hell, but rose from the dead.**

   ◆ We acknowledge that the Son of God offered up His life to show us that God can bring salvation out of shame, deliverance out of disgrace, and life out of death.

   ◆ We dare to believe that Jesus came to present a God of limitless love and that His death was a demonstration of it.

   ◆ We proclaim that to experience the unbounded love of God, we, too, must learn to die and rise again.

4. **We believe that Jesus Christ ascended into heaven to return to God's side, and that He will come again to judge the living and the dead.**

   ◆ We declare that Jesus returned to the Father to show us that heaven is our home and to ready it for our arrival.

   ◆ We believe that Jesus knows our suffering, temptations, and trials, and that He came to call sinners. He alone is our judge. And we trust that the day of judgment is a day of hope, joy, and mercy.

5. **We believe in the Holy Spirit.**

   ◆ We believe that God is Spirit living with us, in us, and for us.

   ◆ We affirm that the Spirit is *holy*. The Spirit does not destroy. The Spirit creates, makes whole, leads us to faith and to God. The Spirit makes *us* holy.

   ◆ We declare that God loves us so much, that He gives us not only the Son, but His own Spirit, to inspire, support, and help us respond to God's love.

6. **We believe in the holy catholic Church.**

   ◆ We profess that the Church is the People of God trying to respond and witness to

A LITTLE CATECHISM: BELIEVE

# WE BELIEVE

God's great love by taking the message of Jesus seriously and living it out together.

◆ We declare that the Church is catholic, a believing community that is open to everybody and in which there can be no outcasts.

◆ We are convinced that the Church is the sign of the Good News of Christ for the world and that our service reveals God's love.

7. **We believe in the communion of saints.**

◆ We believe that all people, living and dead, who are followers of Jesus, belong to a great circle of friends starting with Mary, the Mother of God and our Mother. All these people trust and cherish Jesus as He trusts and cherishes us.

◆ We declare that we are united with all believers in every time and place.

8. **We believe in the forgiveness of sins.**

◆ We declare that the lives of those who follow Jesus revolve around forgiveness.

◆ We believe that our loving, gracious God is also a God of mercy.

◆ We witness to God's forgiving love by seeking and offering forgiveness.

9. **We believe in the resurrection of the body and life everlasting.**

◆ We declare that rising with Christ means we will have new life with Him forever— in body and spirit, mind and feelings.

◆ We believe that heaven is our home, and by following Jesus and being faithful, we will live there in joy for eternity.

## Sacred Scripture in the Life of the Community

The Word of God is so powerful that it supports us in all aspects of our belief. It is our first nourishment. Every follower of Jesus should be familiar with Sacred Scripture—both the Hebrew Scriptures and the Christian Testament.

1. The Bible is the history of God's action in human life. It is also the story of Christ from the moment of creation through the activities of the first Christians.

2. The Sacred Scriptures contain the Word of God and are truly inspired.

3. God is the author of Sacred Scripture because it is the Holy Spirit who inspired its human authors. The Bible teaches God's unfailing truth.

4. As Catholics we believe that any interpretation of the inspired Scripture is a matter of the Church's faithful teaching down through the ages.

5. The four Gospels are the center and core of Sacred Scripture, because Jesus Christ is the Center of the Gospels.

6. Anyone who would follow Jesus needs to learn to do the following:

◆ Read the Scripture!
◆ Understand the Scripture!
◆ Love the Scripture!
◆ Pray the Scripture!
◆ Live the Scripture!

Believe

# FAITH IS LIKE . . .

Along each of the following continuum lines, draw a circle to show which of the two words or phrases better describes the way you would complete each sentence. Then explain yourself.

1. I think faith is like
   work ———————— play

   _____
   _____

2. When it comes to deciding what's important about life, faith is
   an obstacle ———————— an advantage

   _____
   _____
   _____

3. I believe that the best way to share faith is by talking about it ———————— living it

   _____
   _____

4. I think faith means acting
   somber ———————— lighthearted

   _____
   _____

5. To live a rewarding life, I think faith is
   unnecessary ———————— essential

   _____
   _____

6. I think faith is
   a gift ———————— earned

   _____
   _____

Now answer the following questions for yourself:

◆ Do you think it is important to have faith? Why or why not?

   _____
   _____

◆ Do you have faith in yourself? Why or why not?

   _____
   _____

◆ Who has faith in you? Why?

   _____
   _____

◆ What is the one thing about your Christian faith that challenges you the most? Why?

   _____
   _____

◆ What is the one thing about your Christian faith that comforts you most? Why?

   _____
   _____

# THE SLOANS WERE UP TO SOMETHING

Grandpa George Sloan swung back and forth in the hammock that hung between the two birch trees in the backyard. Grandpa George's old fishing hat was pulled down over his eyes. His hands were crossed over his round tummy. A glass of lemonade sat next to him on a small patio table. An airplane zoomed overhead. Cars whisked past out in the street. Bees buzzed around the glass of lemonade. But Grandpa George hardly moved a muscle. He just kept swinging back and forth in the hammock. The Sloans were up to something wonderfully refreshing and renewing.

Uncle Wayne Sloan sat at a card table that was covered with many tiny pieces of plastic. Slowly and carefully, he began to fit the pieces together with glue. Uncle Wayne paid careful attention to what he was doing. He didn't look up, and he didn't look down. Little by little, with Uncle Wayne's care, the many tiny pieces became one, whole, model boat. The Sloans were up to something wonderfully imaginative and creative.

## Something in the Air

Grandma Betty Sloan hummed to herself as she moved around the kitchen. She filled the sink with peelings from crisp apples. She sliced the peeled apples, sprinkled them with sugar and cinnamon, wrapped them in crust, and popped them into the oven. Soon the sweet, warm smell of apple pie filled Grandma Betty's kitchen. The Sloans were up to something wonderfully welcoming and hospitable.

Dad and Mom Sloan sat on the couch with Janet and Julie. They all were looking at an old photo album. Dad and Mom shared memories about the pictures in the album. Janet and Julie asked lots of questions about the "olden days."

The Sloans were up to something wonderfully caring and loving.

## More than a Meal

At six o'clock, all the Sloans gathered around the dining room table. Together, they gave thanks to God. They shared stories and laughter. They served one another the delicious food Grandma Betty had prepared. The Sloans were up to something wonderfully nourishing and sustaining.

When dinner was over, Grandpa George patted his round belly, and everyone laughed. Uncle Wayne showed off his model boat, and everyone clapped. Grandma Betty brought out her dessert of sweet apple pie, and everyone cheered. Janet and Julie asked everyone if they could have more days like this, and everyone promised, "Yes!" The Sloans were up to something wonderfully praiseworthy and promising.

The Sloans were up to celebrating.

*Celebrate*

# FAITH IS CELEBRATED

Everything we believe is part of a celebration of worship, sacrament, and sacrifice.

## Why We Celebrate

Christians have a sixth sense. Faith in Jesus' coming, life, death, and resurrection helps us recognize that all things are God-touched. That recognition fills us with gratefulness for the bounty that surrounds us. And so we give thanks for all things, the bright and the beautiful, the bleak and the bare. We express our appreciation in celebration—in *worship.*

Our worship tells us that in even the most ordinary of days and seasons, people and events, things and actions, there is something extraordinary. Our worship reveals that there is more to life than meets the eye. That is why neither preaching, nor catechesis; neither social justice, nor peace on earth, but celebration—worship, or liturgy—is the *first* "work" of God's People.

## How We Celebrate

We celebrate with visible signs of God's love. (We call it *grace.*) We call these signs "sacraments"—signs make real what they signify. Knowing this, believing this, is crucial. Why? Because real life is lived by signs. A handshake seals reconciliation. A hug banishes fears. A kiss is a promise. Without signs, love has no language. Jesus knew this. That is why Jesus chose *actions* and *gestures* (washing, eating, feeding, touching) to be *signs* of God's love. When we celebrate the sacraments, we make Christ's actions our actions.

Each sacrament is a joyous sign/action in which we join to celebrate our shared experience of God's love for us in Jesus. When we celebrate a sacrament, we grow closer to one another and to God who is present among us. A sacrament is never a private thing. It's an action of a community. We believe that Jesus gave us seven sacraments:

1. *Baptism:* The waters of Baptism reveal the life-giving power of God. In those same waters, we die and rise with Christ and become members of God's life-giving Church.

2. *Confirmation:* The laying on of hands and anointing of Confirmation reveal the Spirit of God's strengthening power. By these same signs, we experience the gift of God's Holy Spirit.

3. *Eucharist:* The gathering, storytelling, thanking, and the eating of the Eucharist reveal the saving presence and action of God's love made flesh on our behalf. Our sharing in the Eucharist is a sharing in the very Body and Blood of Christ, who gave Himself for us on the cross.

4. *Reconciliation:* The welcome, sharing, and absolution of the sacrament of Reconciliation (also called Penance) reveal that God is a God of mercy and ultimate concern. Our celebration of Reconciliation forgives our sins, reunites us with the Lord, and empowers us to reconcile with others.

5. *Anointing of the Sick:* The anointing and healing touch of the sacrament of Anointing of the Sick reveal the healing power of God. Through this sacrament, we experience the sensitive, strengthening, and healing touch of Christ and the compassionate care of the Church.

A LITTLE CATECHISM: CELEBRATE

6. *Holy Orders:* The laying on of hands in the sacrament of Holy Orders reveals Christ's promise and commitment to ongoing leadership and service that will enable us to know and proclaim the gospel, celebrate the sacraments, witness to the risen Lord, and reach out in service to one another. Through this sacrament, bishops, priests, and deacons are ordained to guide, enliven, and serve God's People.

7. *Matrimony:* The commitment to lasting faithfulness made in the sacrament of Matrimony reveals Christ's faithful love for the Church. The couple who celebrate this sacrament are bound together in Christ's faithful love for as long as they live.

## Grace, Sacraments, and You

Our celebration of the sacraments gives us *grace.* Grace is another name for a sharing in God's own life and friendship. In worship and in the sacraments, we share in the graced community, which is the Church.

From all eternity God has loved you. God asks but one thing, that you love in return. God went so far as to become a human being, Jesus Christ, to show you how to love. Because of Jesus' coming, all the ordinary things of life—a bath, a rubbing with oil, a meal, a hug—now have the power to reveal God's love for you.

## Days of Wonder—Days of Joy

Christians have always held Sunday as a day of rest, of celebration, and of prayer. It is the day of Christ's Resurrection. The community requires of its members that we celebrate the Easter mystery every Sunday. Sunday is the most important day

to gather, to listen to God's Word being read in the assembly, and to share in the Lord's Supper.

But the Church also uses the rhythm of the seasons to help us celebrate the mysteries which feed and sustain us in our journey in Jesus's footsteps. We call this the *Church Year:*

1. The year begins with the First Sunday of Advent. Advent means waiting for the coming of Jesus, the Savior, in the Christmas Feast. The color of the season is purple—a sign of penance and waiting.

2. Christmas and Epiphany celebrate the wonders surrounding the birth of Jesus—the love of His family, the hopes and expectations of the world that needs Him so much. The color of Christmas is the white of pure joy.

3. Lent is a time for renewal, prayer, study, and hope. It is a time to prepare for the feast of the Resurrection. It is a time for penance and forgiveness. The color of these forty days is the purple of penance and waiting.

4. Easter celebrates the most important wonder of the whole Christian Faith—Christ is risen! This feast and the weeks that follow have a song that is sung over and over. *Alleluia!* That means "Shout with joy!" Jesus had defeated sin and death. We will live forever! The season ends with Pentecost—the coming of the Holy Spirit. The color of Easter is joyful white. The color of Pentecost is fiery red.

5. Ordinary Time is celebrated in the other weeks of the year. The cold of mid-winter and the balmy days of summer usually fall in Ordinary Time. These Sundays show that every time is God's time. The color of Ordinary Time is the green of hope and peace.

CHRISTIAN INITIATION

# CELEBRATE THE MOMENTS OF YOUR LIFE

On a separate sheet of paper, create a time line that notes important events or moments in your life (for example, birth, moving to a new house or town, winning an award, death of a family member). Write how you celebrated (or continue to celebrate) those moments.

## Jesus the Celebrator

Read the entire Gospel according to Luke. Don't panic. You don't have to read it all in one sitting. In Jesus' words, actions, and stories, note how often he speaks about celebration and/or celebrates Himself. Use the space below to jot down what you discover.

## The Celebrating Parish

Rate your parish **P** for Poor, **F** for Fair, or **G** for Good on how well you think it celebrates . . .

_____ welcome and belonging

_____ the presence of God's Spirit

_____ serving and caring

_____ forgiveness

_____ healing

_____ leadership

_____ faithfulness and love

## Personal Questions

◆ Does your parish try to make you feel welcome and involved in its celebration?

_____

◆ What do you like best about the way your parish celebrates?

_____

◆ What do you like least about the way your parish celebrates?

_____

A LITTLE CATECHISM: CELEBRATE

# FAITH-IN-ACTION

**The Church of Christ the Savior** in Zacamil, El Salvador, is a very poor community—as poor as can be. Twice the village has been destroyed by army troops who resented the work and struggle of the poor people there. The community is divided into small groups (called *base communities*). These groups support their members, care for them, comfort them, encourage them, and even feed them. Together they pray for freedom and a better life. Together they hope. When the people of Christ the Savior were asked to tell the story of their lives, they did it in the form of a creed—a statement of faith. Here is what these people say about themselves.

**WE BELIEVE in God,** who created us free and walks with us in the struggle for freedom.

**WE BELIEVE in Christ,** crucified again in the suffering of the poor, a suffering which calls out to the conscience of people and nations, a suffering which ends in resurrection.

**WE BELIEVE in the power of the Spirit,** capable of inspiring the same compassion which has led our best brothers and sisters to suffering and death.

**WE BELIEVE in the Church,** called forth by Jesus and the Holy Spirit.

**WE BELIEVE that when we gather,** Jesus is with us, and Mary, our Mother, is at our side as a sign of faithfulness to the Lord.

**WE BELIEVE in the Christian community,** where we proclaim our ideals, through which we practice our Christian faith.

**WE BELIEVE in building a Church,** where we pray and reflect on our lives, and share in the teaching, worshiping, and caring mission of Jesus. In this way, we make the kingdom of God present on earth.

**WE BELIEVE in unity** in the midst of differences.

**WE BELIEVE that Christ calls us** to communion and to live as sisters and brothers.

**WE BELIEVE that we need to love one another,** to correct one another compassionately, to forgive each other's errors and weaknesses.

**WE BELIEVE that we need to help one another** recognize our limitations, to support each other in the Faith.

**WE BELIEVE that the poor,** the illiterate and the sick, the persecuted and tortured, are closest to the Gospel of Jesus. Through them, Christ challenges us to work for justice and peace. Their cause is our cause.

**WE BELIEVE that Christ is also present** in those who are slaves to their passions, to vices, lies and injustice, to power and money.

**WE COMMIT ourselves to never give up hope** in the possibility of their conversion; to love them even though they slander, persecute and kill us; to pray for them and to help them so that one day they may live simply and humbly in the way the Gospel calls all of us to live.

(From *A Spring Whose Waters Never Run Dry*, EPIC, 1990)

The people of Zacamil, El Salvador may be poor, but they are rich in their understanding of how everyone who answers God's call needs to live faith every day.

# Live

# THE LAW OF LOVE

One day a man asked Jesus what was necessary to live as a faithful person. Jesus responded by telling him to live according to the Law of Love.

> The Lord your God is Lord alone! You must love the Lord your God with all your heart, with all your soul, with all your mind, and with all your strength. And you must love your neighbor as yourself.       (MATTHEW 22:37–39)

Jesus' Law of Love tells that the life of faith is an adventure, not an investment. It calls us to love as God loves. And how does God love? God's love is for everyone. God's love reaches out to those least capable of returning it. God's love has no strings attached. Living lives of faithful love is not easy. But we believe that we have lots of help to do what is right:

1. *Conscience:* Conscience is a gift to help all live good and faithful lives. Conscience is the judgment of what is right and what is wrong. Remember, conscience doesn't work all by itself. The faithful Christian needs to train and teach his or her conscience. The Law of God, the teaching of Jesus, and the help of the Church all come together to help people know what is right and what is wrong.

2. *The Ten Commandments:* God gave the Commandments as a gift—a gift to help people stay faithful.

    ◆ **The First Commandment:** *I am the Lord your God. You shall not have any other gods besides me.* The first commandment reminds us: "Put first things first." And God is to be first in our lives. We cannot allow other things such as money, celebrity, pleasure, or even knowledge to take God's place (to become false gods) in our lives.

    ◆ **The Second Commandment:** *You shall not take the name of the Lord, your God, in vain.* If we say, "I believe in God," but act as if we don't, we're taking the Lord's name in vain. Too many people have "God" on their lips, but "Me" in their hearts. Believing in God should make a difference in the way we live, act, and speak.

    ◆ **The Third Commandment:** *Remember to keep holy the Sabbath Day.* This command calls us to remember that, since God has first loved us, God deserves our devotion, our thanks, and praise. We demonstrate that devotion by worshiping God as individuals and as a people.

    ◆ **The Fourth Commandment:** *Honor your father and your mother.* This commandment tells us that we are related to family, others, and God. It calls us to honor and respect the human condition and those whose love brought us into it and sustain us in it. The fourth commandment is a call to be open-hearted, even soft-hearted toward others. Hard-hearted people are closed to others. Only soft-hearted people can accept the invitation to love.

    ◆ **The Fifth Commandment:** *You shall not kill.* This commandment tells us that life is a God-given gift to be respected and never taken away from others, from the unborn child to the oldest member of the community. This commandment also urges us to work for justice and to strive for peace.

A LITTLE CATECHISM: LIVE

# THE LAW OF LOVE
*Live*

◆ **The Sixth, Ninth, and Tenth Commandments:** *You shall not commit adultery. You shall not covet your neighbor's house. You shall not covet your neighbor's wife.* These commandments teach that human sexual love needs to be expressed only in marriage. It also teaches that attitudes are as important as actions in dealing with others.

◆ **The Seventh and Eighth Commandments:** *You shall not steal. You shall not bear false witness against your neighbor.* Lying, cheating, self-seeking, gossiping, taking what belongs to others, putting oneself first, all are wrong—no matter how common these kinds of actions are.

3. *The Beatitudes:* Jesus offered some special helps for doing what is right. They are called the Beatitudes and they are found in the Gospel of MATTHEW (5:3–11). They also help Christians know how to live their faith.

◆ **Blessed are the poor in spirit, for theirs is the kingdom of heaven.** We need God and the support of others. To recognize our neediness, we must have a poverty of spirit that rejects selfishness and seeks the good of others.

◆ **Blessed are they who mourn, for they will be comforted.** This beatitude reminds us that suffering is part of what it means to be human. Jesus wants us to understand that our suffering, like His, can open our hearts to others and their suffering.

◆ **Blessed are the meek, for they shall possess the land.** Meekness is strength tamed by love. The meek are generous. They have nothing to lose. They don't force themselves on others.

◆ **Blessed are they who hunger and thirst for righteousness, for they will be satisfied.** People who hunger and thirst for righteousness are people who crave the truth. They don't take the easy way out. And so, they are the most satisfied.

◆ **Blessed are the merciful, for they will be shown mercy.** This beatitude tells us that mercy is a permanent way of viewing the world around us. It means viewing and treating the world and all in it with compassion.

◆ **Blessed are the pure of heart, for they will see God.** The pure of heart are single-minded people. They are focused outward, not inward. That open outlook gives them every opportunity to discover God in everything and everyone they see.

◆ **Blessed are the peacemakers, for they shall be called children of God.** Jesus knew that everyone seeks and admires peace. Jesus wanted his followers to do something about it. Peacemakers face the difficulties of building solid relationships between human beings head-on.

◆ **Blessed are they who are persecuted for the sake of righteousness, for theirs is the kingdom of heaven.** The final beatitude reminds us that living out our faith often means appearing foolish in the eyes of others. With a smile, we continue to walk in the way of the Lord.

# *Live* TAKING FAITH "PERSONALLY"

Christians don't simply believe in a set of laws, concepts, or precepts. Christians believe in a person. The core of Christianity is the person of Jesus. In fact, Jesus was so "true" a person He could say that He was truth in the flesh: "I am the truth" (JOHN 14:6).

Notice that Jesus said, "I am" the truth, not "I have" the truth. "I have the truth" is a formula. Lots of people have said, "I have the truth." Only one person has said, "I am the truth." For Jesus, the truth is not a theory. It's a person, and only the personal matters. Only a person is worthy of faith.

For Christians, faith in Jesus means that He is the driving force in our lives. Is Jesus in the driver's seat in your life?

## Have You Driven with the Lord Lately?

In the space provided, design your faith journey. You can use any images, pictures, words, symbols—anything at all. Use the following list to give you some get-started ideas:

1. Depict what you feel is the core or heart of your Christian faith—what drives you.
2. Show an action you have taken that was prompted by your faith.
3. Use three or four words to describe the sort of faithful person you believe you are today.
4. Portray a person of faith-in-action who has inspired your growth in faith.
5. Show a faith action you take that identifies you to others as a Catholic Christian.

# THE CLOWN OF NOTRE DAME

Pray

The clown stood outside the great cathedral of Notre Dame in Paris. Every now and then he would make a face or turn a cartwheel or do a somersault or juggle his pins to entertain the people who were going in and out of the cathedral. And every now and then, one of the people might stop, laugh, and toss him a coin.

The clown knew that the people were all going into the cathedral to pray. Some days he felt that he should be going there, too, but he never did. After all, he did not have the right clothes to go into such a beautiful place. And besides, once inside, what would he do? No one had ever taught him how to pray.

The clown didn't know what words to say. He didn't know if he should stand or kneel or sit. Still, the longer the clown remained outside the cathedral, the stronger he felt about going inside. At last, the feeling became so powerful, the clown couldn't resist it any more, so one afternoon, he quietly slipped inside the cathedral.

The place was crowded with people. Together and alone, they were praying. Soft and loud, they were praying. All around him, they were praying. The clown felt foolish and stupid. He didn't know how to pray. He felt like running away and hiding in the darkest corner of the cathedral. So that is what he did.

The clown sat in the gloomy corner and wept. "How foolish and stupid I must look," he thought to himself. "A clown crying!" The clown cried himself to sleep. When he awoke, it was late at night, and the huge cathedral was locked and empty.

The clown looked for a way out, but could find none. Then he saw a light. It was a candle burning next to a statue of Mary, holding the child Jesus in her arms. The Lady and the child were so beautiful. Yet, the clown's heart felt so empty. He wanted to pray, to thank God for the beautiful Lady and her child. He wanted to pray, but he didn't know how.

But he did know how to clown. So the clown did what he knew how to do. He picked up his pins and began to juggle. Then he turned wonderful somersaults, perfect cartwheels. He made the funniest faces he knew. Faster and faster, he went, until he could go no faster, until he was so tired, he dropped to the floor and fell sound asleep.

Then something amazing happened. The clown didn't see it. In fact, no one saw it, but it happened all the same. The statue of Mary and the child Jesus moved. The child in Mary's arms smiled and clapped His hands. Then Mary bent down and lovingly touched the sleeping clown's smiling face.

"What a wonderful prayer," she whispered.

CHRISTIAN INITIATION

# WHAT IS PRAYER?

**PRAYER** is what happens when people are struck by and respond to the wonder of God's presence, a presence recognized in simple ways:

◆ in deeds of kindness
◆ in the enjoyment of others
◆ in longing, frustration, joy, and pain

Real prayer never happens apart from life. That is why prayer is more than simply talking to God or even pouring our heart and soul out to God. Prayer is responding to God's love and finding the way to God whether the heart is full or empty.

Jesus knew this. He prayed in times of fullness and in times of emptiness. Jesus showed that prayer is the art of Christians.

## When Is the Time for Prayer?

Followers of Jesus are a people of prayer. We are heirs to a rhythm of prayer that is formed by the lives of people who are special to us, and that is as ordinary as the pages of the calendar and the hours on the clock.

1. *We can pray seasonally.* Each of the seasons we celebrate (Advent, Christmas, Lent, Easter, Ordinary Time) has its special flavor and feel.

2. *We can pray to remember and celebrate others.* Our lives have all been touched by the lives and example of others—heroes and heroines, family members, saints. The Church gives us prayers to the saints (for example, the "Hail, Mary") and saints' days to remember these people (for example, St. Lucy on December 13, St. Joseph on March 19), but we can also devise our own saints' calendar to remember the "saints" who are special to us, our family and friends.

3. *We can pray weekly.* The rhythm of the week, especially that established by Sunday, surrounds our lives. We begin each week with a grand prayer celebration that shapes all other days of our week.

4. *We can pray at life's special moments.* This means that the rhythm of life also summons our prayer. Conceiving, giving birth, caring, nourishing, gathering, departing, hurting, healing, dying—all mark important points in our lives. Prayer at these times allows us to marvel at life's rhythms and to thank God for them and for all of life.

5. *We can pray daily.* Think of a normal day: We awake, wash, eat, work, play, share, rest, sleep. For centuries God's people have recognized God's presence in this "daily" rhythm and responded in prayer (for example, Liturgy of the Hours).

## Where Do We Pray?

Just as having a place to play encourages us to play, so does having a place for prayer sway us to pray. The faith community has such a place, the parish church. However, there is no perfect or right place to pray. It's just important that you have your own personal place for prayer, and you can find it in your own home.

1. *Create a "special" place in your home for prayer.* At different times or seasons of the year, you can make a special place for prayer in your home. During Advent, you can place an Advent wreath to mark that place. During Lent, you may erect a cross. During the Easter season, let a large candle designate your place.

# WHAT IS PRAYER?

2. *The family table is a place for prayer.* Even over spilt milk and warnings of, "Finish your vegetables, or no dessert," the family table is the place where all take time to come together for nourishment. At the family table, we serve one another and are served. At the family table, we share how much we mean to one another and how much we need one another. The family table is a wonderful place for prayer.

3. *The bed or bedside is a place for prayer.* Bedtime is more than sleep time. In bed is where we are born, rested, renewed, and where most of us die. In bed, we have some of our finest ideas and scariest fears. Prayer in bed or at our bedside is prayer that touches us where we live and die.

4. *A private place is a place for prayer.* The Scriptures tell us that Jesus often went off to a private place to pray. You can find your own private place to pray, away from the distractions and noise. There, you can do what Jesus so often did—be alone with God.

## How Should We Pray?

This is not an easy question to answer. Just as there is no "perfect" or "right" *place* to pray, so too, there is no "perfect" or "right" *way* to pray. In fact, our Christian tradition tells us that there are many ways to pray.

1. *Pray with words.* This may seem obvious, because when we think of prayer, we generally think of the words of prayers we know. Words in prayer hint at things, like words in poetry. They open our imagination. The words of prayer can also act as rallying points, drawing people together like cheers (for example, "Amen!" or "Alleluia!"). You can find words like these in the Bible (God's Word to us). Look to the stories, the "once upon a times" of the Gospels, and to the words of Jesus Himself.

2. *Pray with silence.* Silence is more than the absence of words. Silence has its own voice and can be a positive presence. Silence in prayer is especially appropriate when we don't have the words to pray or don't know what to pray for. Silence allows us to shut up and let God's Spirit do the talking.

3. *Pray with the help of objects.* The Church teaches that sacramentals (objects such as rosaries, crucifixes, statues, and the like) are reminders of God's presence. They can also help us to pray and to focus on God as our center.

4. *Pray with your whole self.* Our tradition reminds us that we are a body people: a people who dance, sing, dunk, throw water around, splash, anoint, create smells, light fires, stand, bow, bend, kneel, swallow, drink, chew, reach, clap, look one another in the eye, hug, and touch. Using our bodies in prayer—like the clown of Notre Dame—puts conviction into our prayer and prayer into our bones.

CHRISTIAN INITIATION

# CREATE YOUR OWN PRAYER

You can pray any way you want: with words, silence, objects, and gestures. This page is a canvas for you to paint your prayer. If you'd like to create a prayer with words, you can use the Church's traditional structure in the outline below. The rest is up to you!

1. Begin by addressing your prayer to God.
   FOR EXAMPLE: *Loving Father* or *Gracious God.*

2. Communicate your feelings, usually by offering thanks for God's gifts to you.
   FOR EXAMPLE: *Your generous kindness has called me to faith.*

3. Ask for continued blessing.
   FOR EXAMPLE: *Help my unbelief and lead me to ever greater trust in You.*

4. Conclude by wrapping your prayer in Jesus' name.
   FOR EXAMPLE: *I ask this through Christ Jesus, the Lord. Amen.*

# The Lord's Prayer

Jesus wanted us to know that prayer is not really what we ask of God, but the way we respond to what God asks of us. Prayer is our answer to God's call to grow in love. Prayer doesn't make God care about us, because God *already* cares about us. Prayer makes us become caring about God, about God's will for us, and about others in all we say and do.

Jesus knew that to pray like this, we had to learn more than what prayer to pray. We had to learn what kind of prayer to be. That is why Jesus taught us to pray . . .

> Our Father, who art in heaven, hallowed be Thy name; Thy Kingdom come; Thy will be done on earth as it is in heaven. Give us this day our daily bread; and forgive us our trespasses as we forgive those who trespass against us; and lead us not into temptation, but deliver us from evil.
>
> (Based on LUKE 11:2–4)

## Our Father, who art in heaven, hallowed be Thy name.

Jesus wanted us to put first things first in our prayer. That is why when Jesus taught us to pray, He said to pray like children to a loving parent who knows what we need and who will take care of us. In teaching us to address God as "Father," Jesus draws on our understanding and experience of what it means to be a loving parent—identifying it with God's overwhelming concern for us—and demonstrates how bold and how intimate we may be in our prayer. At the same time, Jesus shows what our prayer will accomplish, namely, the sanctification of God's name.

## Thy Kingdom come; Thy will be done on earth as it is in heaven.

Then Jesus teaches us to pray as He prays: to put God's will and the coming of God's kingdom first. He calls us to set our hearts on God's kingdom before all else. Praying that way guarantees that we'll end up praying for all else as a means of paving the way for the kingdom's coming.

## Give us this day our daily bread;

God knows everything we need. Even so, Jesus wants us to remember that God cares about our everyday life. So Jesus also teaches us to share our needs with God.

## and forgive us our trespasses as we forgive those who trespass against us;

Jesus, then, reminds us that if we pray for the coming of God's kingdom, we also must pray to act like people of God's kingdom.

## and lead us not into temptation, but deliver us from evil.

Finally, Jesus ends His teaching the way He began. Jesus reminds us that we are children of a loving God. Like children, we need a parent's help. We need a parent's caring love.

# A CERTIFICATE OF
# *Belonging*

This is to certify that

(Name) _____


has participated in the Benziger *Christian Initiation* experience:

◆ listening with heart and soul

◆ sharing with others longings and fears

◆ connecting faith with everyday life

◆ trying to learn attitudes, skills, and actions

◆ supporting others who participated in this time of growth and love

Therefore, this certificate recognizes the great gift of belonging to God's Family—The Church!


Given by the Community of _____
                                                                (name of parish)

(Signed) _____